What others have to say about
My Butterfly Mind

Informative and illuminating. *My Butterfly Mind* explores the reality of living with dyslexia and dyspraxia from a personal perspective. This vivid autobiographical story has many compelling anecdotes and experiences that give insight into these conditions. Undiagnosed for three decades, Claire Moore's candid life story informs as well as entertains by exemplifying the physical, emotional, social and psychological challenges she faced with courage and final self-acceptance.

Helen Cerne MA, PhD.

My Butterfly Mind is on a very topical issue — children with dyslexia and dyspraxia and the hurdles they face, from the point of view of someone who herself is a person with dyslexia and dyspraxia. It demonstrates beautifully the problems — not just physical but also emotional, psychological and societal — that these children face throughout their lives. They are rarely understood, often treated cruelly — whether deliberately or not — and feel they are a burden to all. The author uses her own experiences to demonstrate these challenges and how she has overcome the barriers that society had, often unwittingly, put in her path. She is positive throughout, even in negative situations, and shows how obstacles can be overcome with determination and a positive attitude.

Dyslexia and dyspraxia are permanent features of a person's life. The author demonstrates how to live with them as comfortably as possible, how to overcome limitations and find different ways and means to get around the problems that people with dyslexia and dyspraxia face constantly.

This book is important for all people who interact with these children — especially parents, teachers and caregivers — to read to gain a greater awareness of how the problems affect the children throughout their lives. It should be made mandatory for all special needs teachers and organisations.

I highly recommend this book to all who have even a nodding acquaintance with dyslexia and dyspraxia. It is easy to read and interesting throughout.

Sophia Z Kovachevich MA Eng. Lit., MA Eng. Ling.; BA Pol. Sc., BA World History, BA Comparative Cultures; PhD (incl. in Lit., Ling. Theology); Dip. in TESOL, Dip. in Proofreading and Editing, Dip. in Aromatherapy

My Butterfly Mind

MY BUTTERFLY MIND

Insights into dyslexia and dyspraxia

CLAIRE MOORE

First published 2023

Copyright © Claire Moore 2023

All rights reserved. No part of this publication may be reproduced, stored in a retrieval system or transmitted in any form by any means, electronic, mechanical, photocopying, recording or otherwise, without the prior written permission of the publisher and copyright holder. Claire Moore asserts the moral right to be identified as the author of this work.

Cover design and typesetting by BookPOD

Typeset in Dyslexie 9/16

ISBN: 978-0-6459317-0-9 (paperback)
eISBN: 978-0-6459317-1-6 (ebook)

A catalogue record for this book is available from the National Library of Australia

This book is typeset in a font named Dyslexie. This font has been specially designed for people with dyslexia — which enhances the ease of reading and comprehension.

Contents

Preface 1
Introduction 3
Dyslexia 8
Clues and Salvation 13
Butterfly Mind 15
Dyslexia and Dyspraxia Symptoms 17
Dyspraxia 21
Living with Dyslexia and Dyspraxia 23
Aged Three 27
Aged Four 32
Ascot Vale West State School 35
Grade Four 37
Beginnings 39
Grade Four, Dyspraxia Manifests 42
Grade Five, Ascot Vale West School 47
Nan 50
Penleigh 53

Sport	59
Dyspraxia Strikes	62
Undiagnosed Dyspraxia	64
Denial of Dyslexia	67
All Saints Church, Ascot Vale	69
Sunday School Picnics	72
Holy Trinity Anglican Church	74
Words as Symbols	76
Language	81
Appreciating the Music of Words	83
Other Languages	85
Pianos and Other Matters	88
Binoculars and Other Matters	92
Gambling	95
Odds and Sods	97
University	99
Dyslexia and Learning	101
Promotion	103
Parental Patterns	105
Ritual Meals at Newmarket	110
Growing Up	116
Shattered Elbow	120
Living with Dyspraxia	123
Dyspraxia and the Bank	129
Questions That May Help after a Fall	133
Dyspraxia Theory	135

Helping Teenagers and Adults With Dyslexia .. 136
Undiagnosed Dyslexia in Others 140
More Symptoms of Dyslexia 145
Respectability 147
Left and Right Hand, Which Side Is Which? ... 148
Not Listening 150
The Joy of Computers 152
Digital Delights 155
Filing Follies 157
Unanswered Questions 159
My Writing 162
Blessings 164
Acknowledgements 168
Bibliography 170

Preface

Researching and writing your family history, autobiography or memoir is always challenging. But if you're dyslexic and dyspraxic like Claire Moore, you need even more determination.

Unusual problem solving has always intrigued me and especially the original ways in which some people think or tackle their writing challenges as a way of sharing important ideas or experiences. Claire joined my 'Complete Your Book in a Year' writing workshop at the Public Records Office in North Melbourne. She struggled but always did her homework. She finished her first family history book project *A Family Jigsaw*, about juggling the ancestors (including one who was a professional juggler), then *Broken Links* using poems to characterise her ancestors' links and lives. This was an economic way to convey the essence of the big cast of her family and circumvent her dyslexic expression.

Claire now uses poetry as a technique to link facts with emotion.

Her best poem for quick characterisation was 'Blacksmithing 1850s', which portrayed Willy her blacksmith ancestor.

Her 'poetic' format was an innovation for family history writing and could help others, especially if they were dealing with big numbers and many generations.

I had a working knowledge of dyslexia but no real understanding of her specific issues until the 'Dyslexia' poem in her fourth work which arrived in the mail, *Poems from a Butterfly Mind: Dyslexia and Dyspraxia, Both Obscure, Dance with Family Dysfunction.*

Using poems as a way of explaining the essence of her history, is a kind of shorthand.

My poem to Claire after reading her manuscript:

> Butterfly Mind,
> Like an Impressionist painter
> Autobiography in word sketches
> Raw emotions, captured,
> Juxtaposed,
> On paper.
> Others have only the challenges of spell check and procrastination.

Hazel Edwards
Author
Patron: Society of Women Writers Vic.
2022 Monash University Distinguished Alumni Award for Education

Introduction

There is no escaping symptoms of dyslexia with dyspraxia as they twist through my mind and body. Undiagnosed, they stalked me in many areas of my life. My mother and father are referred to as Molly and Fred as this provides me with objectivity. They knew me to be intelligent. Never-ending falls and co-ordination problems were ignored.

Girls in our family and within the wider community were treated differently to boys. Dyslexic women, often ignored, more easily fall into traps of limited education and job opportunities.

My first teacher announced that dyslexic children often turned b's, d's and p's around the wrong way when writing. This was easy for me to do. Concentration on not doing so became a priority. Writing in school was a wearying chore. Telling no one. Ignoring my first clues.

How impossible to unravel dyslexia and dyspraxia symptoms when ignorant of both. Undiagnosed symptoms of dyspraxia and dyslexia changed my life. Limiting opportunities while stifling movements. Creating challenges that my butterfly mind uses to change experiences.

Demonstrating how these challenges unravelled within my life. Diagnoses brought understanding, increasing the ability of my butterfly mind to cope with every challenge.

Discover how dyslexia is more than a reading-spelling problem.

Explore how dyspraxia is more than being clumsy and careless. Fellow sufferers and educationalists may find my journey informative. I want to share how I think and how I cope.

Not being aware of my dyslexia gave me the opportunity to solve challenges from different angles. Dyslexic clues were ignored due to a preoccupation with family fairness and gender conflicts. Discovering my dyspraxia came as a great release, relieving me of constant guilt of clumsiness with the result of disasters being seen as entirely my fault. Early in the 1970s, as a newlywed, confinement to home by spinal issues was unrelentingly boring. Joining a Humanistic Study Course at the now defunct South Melbourne Technical School proved an exciting and energising experience leading to the attending of a speech by the Vice Chancellor of Deakin University. My degree as an off-campus student opened my mind to exciting ideas and realities. The perfect antidote to suburban isolation. Deakin University accepted me as a dyslexic student. The Disability Vera White Centre aided me. An exciting and rewarding experience.

Considering my family life as normal, unravelling the complexities of my nuclear family relationships has aided healing. My mother's nickname was Molly. Fred is an abbreviation of his first name. By using those titles, emotional distance was achieved and objectivity became a reality. This book would not have been possible if I'd called them Mum and Dad.

My writing mentor, Hazel Edwards, suggested that I produce a book about my experience with undiagnosed dyslexia and dyspraxia demonstrating my thought patterns to solve problems created by both conditions. In my poetry book *Poems from A Butterfly Mind: Dyslexia and Dyspraxia Both Obscure, Dance with Family Dysfunction*, material from my past has been used to demonstrate the realities of my early life with dyslexia and dyspraxia.

My stories and poems are not a memoir but an instrument to demonstrate dysfunctional issues such as erratic spelling and continual falls out of consciousness. Plus looking at social norms of the time. The books are for those who have experience of dyslexia and dyspraxia, their parents, siblings and teachers.

Dyslexia has presented me with different challenges to other people. Being undiagnosed until my thirties has been a distinct blessing because I have never thought of myself as disabled. Rather, I use different pathways of learning and reality to normal.

What is normal? Many people, particularly in mainstream education, plus many parents, have difficulty in realising that there are other ways of learning than what is regarded as the norm.

Dyslexia becomes a disability when undiagnosed children are not taught to read through use of phonics or other means.

Disabled? No.

Different? Yes.

Labelling children stunts growth. Ridicule induces shame, compromising use of an individual's inherent abilities. It seems the education system is uninterested in exploring all children's learning abilities.

Dyslexia has affected all my senses except taste and smell.

My speech includes dangling sentences as mentioned elsewhere. My hearing is not always accurate.

MY BUTTERFLY MIND

Dyslexia reinforces problems with co-ordination and balance.

My sense of sight really contributes a great deal to my dyslexia.

Dyslexia

Definition of dyslexia

'The BDA [British Dyslexia Association] has adopted the Rose (2009) definition of dyslexia:

Dyslexia is a learning difficulty that primarily affects the skills involved in accurate and fluent word reading and spelling. Characteristic features of dyslexia are difficulties in phonological awareness, verbal memory and verbal processing speed. Dyslexia occurs across the range of intellectual abilities. It is best thought of as a continuum, not a distinct category, and there are no clear cut-off points. Co-occurring difficulties may be seen in aspects of language, motor co-ordination, mental calculation, concentration and personal organisation, but these are not, by themselves, markers of dyslexia. A good indication of the severity and persistence of dyslexic difficulties can be gained by examining how the individual responds to or has responded to well-founded intervention.'

(Source: https://www.bdadyslexia.org.uk/news/definition-of-dyslexia)

Dyslexia

Individual symptoms
Erratic spelling
Dangling sentences
Verbal or written
(unfinished)
unaware
Dictionaries horror
Left or right disaster
Reading
Time a punt
Sometimes
Incorrect
Father
difficult words
thrown at me
to spell
Success often
Phonics
Salvation
Ears dictate
how to spell
Texting
Crosswords
Scrabble
No fun
No way
Instructions
miss a step
Fail
Can look but not see
Words nonsense
Letters jumble
Stare until sense arrives
Challenges to overcome.

Claire Moore 6/2/2020

Dyslexia seems to have many definitions. There are so many combinations of problems that make up dyslexia. In the worst cases, reading is not possible. These individuals need specialist teaching aides plus oral exams. In America they seem to diagnose and treat dyslexics much better than we here in Victoria. The definition most acceptable to me is that dyslexia occurs when information between left brain and right brain fails to communicate or communicates the wrong way.

Dyspraxia, on the other hand, has been defined as a right dominated brain person living in a left brain dominated world. Dyspraxia, inherited clumsiness, has affected every part of my life.

Often dyslexia is not diagnosed until later in life, particularly in women. My dyslexia was not diagnosed until my thirty-third year.

Weapons against my dyslexia:

A. Molly was a dedicated reader.
B. Molly was a qualified elocutionist, who pronounced syllables and vowels in her spoken speech.
C. My memory was very good.
D. Words that convey images are easy for me to visualise in my mind.

E. My first years in school spelling were taught by phonics. Using phonics tells my ears how to spell.

F. In Bubs, our teacher told us that dyslexics turn Bb's, Dd's and Pp's around. Learning not to do this was one of my first tasks.

G. Words that had no image would trip me up when reading aloud. Learning such words off by heart was the second task.

H. F for Fred and discipline. Verbal strife. Determination.

Words that created images, such as owl, cat, hat, dog, trees, were easy.

My downfall was with words beginning with W. Two 'u's joined together. Where, with, when, were, was, which had to be written down, then learnt by heart. My memory really was phenomenal. Poems, stories in Golden Books, articles from school readers all memorised. Molly read me many Greek myths, including *The Iliad*. All stories were squirrelled away in my brain for further reference.

After dinner every night, Molly and Fred would sit in their armchairs. Either Molly or Fred would read to me, usually Molly, but sometimes Fred. Four years of me sitting on a knee or on a chair arm looking at pictures in books and words that created images seen by my head. Stories fascinated me. After Angus's arrival, we would sit on each side of Molly while she read. Boys' tales were now read, exposing me to *The Air Adventures of Biggles* and other boys' stories.

Stories on the wireless encouraged listening. On the weekend, *The Cruel Sea* was serialised. Behind the lounge door, all could be heard by me, but not understood at all. Television was not around to distract my hearing. Without my hearing, spelling would not exist for me as a child. Failure to read would have meant Molly and Fred would have disowned me! Phonics were my salvation. Reading allowed my brain to absorb the sounds of vowels and syllables. Reading saved me from much of the dysfunctionality of my family. When my nose was in a book, everyone left me alone. All our nuclear family were readers. Molly worried about my spelling.

Clues and Salvation

Living in the outer suburbs of Melbourne with limited transport, no car, no telephone, was not an enjoyable experience. Salvation came in the shape of a Humanistic Study Course at South Melbourne Technical College for six weeks, four mornings a week. I was in ignorance of my dyslexia. After this course, most of our class stayed on to tackle Middle Level English. Several of us passed a Melbourne University English Exam.

Professor Max Charlesworth gave a lecture at South Melbourne Neighbourhood House about mature age students being eligible to study at Deakin University in off-campus programs. Four class members enrolled as external students at Deakin University. My dyslexia, luckily, was diagnosed the year before I was accepted at Deakin.

In the early 1960s, I noticed myself reading headlines that failed to make sense. A rare occurrence. I stared at the headlines until they did make sense. Left and right confusion provided clues along a long trail to my dyslexia. Discovering my dyspraxia took me longer. Co-ordination, balance problems, fingers that failed all put down to clumsiness.

Butterfly Mind

My mind flits from topic to topic, feeling to feeling. Aware of the micro and usually a bigger picture. I am always observing the scene and situations.

Let me share my past. As a sensitive child, it appeared to me that adults did not cope with childish tears. Nor were my desires given consideration, let alone acceptance, by my family. Gender issues were obvious to me from a very young age. Girls were irrelevant. They married or stayed single, became a good aunt, responsible for the care of parents in their old age. Otherwise they married, reproduced children and learnt family patterns.

In poorer families, girls' schooling was often cut short. 'Old maids', as single women were called, were objects of ridicule in our street. They worked and looked after their own business without any help from others. If they carried a leather case, similar to men's, then they were demonised as alcoholics, hiding grog in their case.

Newspapers were a constant in our house. We were expected to read all the papers except *The Truth*, forbidden to read such trash. Fred bought the paper for the racing form guide. The Toorak gossip was interesting. Puzzle pages in the paper are a complete waste of time for me. Sudokus! How people love to give me small books.

'You'll love them. They are so much fun.'

My mind has not got a clue. They are not fun! Who listens? Not a teacher friend who knows I am dyslexic apparently. Many of my friends are addicted to games, mind games like Scrabble or games requiring manual dexterity. Card games after two hands seem so boring. Watching others play games can be entertaining.

Dyslexia and Dyspraxia Symptoms

After successfully completing a course of Western Herbal Medicine, I suddenly discovered keeping records of patients was a hopeless task.

During lessons in Anatomy and Physiology, we had a whole lesson on dyslexia and dyspraxia. Knowing dyslexia affected me, it was a total surprise to discover that dyspraxia was much more of a problem for me than dyslexia.

Some symptoms belong to both. Symptoms were set out as a menu. Dyslexia on the left-hand side, dyspraxia on the right. Dyspraxia symptoms dominated. My co-ordination has always been defective. Falls, concussions, skeletal damage. Not being aware of my body in space. Elbows that knock things off tables and benches.

Large books where the back binding breaks. The more I try to look after bound books, the more they come to grief.

Dyspraxia explained my early inability to move a swing. My climbing failures. Twisting ankles when running. Inward turning hips that created knock knees. One foot turned in, one out. A sporting disaster.

My 500 supervised hours as a herbalist included two public lectures on dyslexia and dyspraxia at a local neighbourhood house. Some parents often restrict dyslexic children instead of encouraging and accepting their individual abilities.

Educational Kinesiology includes Brain Gym, a book of exercises that aids brain integration for dyslexia and dyspraxia affected individuals. Pilates weekly sessions for the last 20 years. Every day combining with Pilates exercises. Ten years ago adding Dragon Gate Chi Gong exercises to my daily routine. Forty to fifty minutes of exercises in the morning. Repeating Chi Gong exercises before bed has kept my body supple, improved my co-ordination and reduced pain experiences. Not to exercise means to lose control of my body movements, increasing uncoordinated movements, which leads to increased falls, resulting in increased pain and stress, encouraging dyslexic chaos and ruining sleep patterns.

To co-ordinate arms and legs, concentration is needed. This can be difficult when dyslexia distracts my attention.

'Always look ahead, never look down, shoulders back when walking.' A recipe for disaster for me. My eyes need to be looking for all obstacles in my path that can be tripped over. Qualified remedial massages fortnightly, acupuncture and naturopathy are all tools to limit pain while keeping me fit. Weak wrists, combined with fingers with little or no sense of touch, ensures childproof objects are usually Claire-proof too. A good can opener is priceless.

Do not talk to me about fitted sheets. Impossible for my hands. Need to buy two sets of sheets to gain two sheets to tuck in easily. Hands that fail to stretch an octave and one when playing the piano. Phones that had dials posed no problem. Button phones one presses are a huge challenge. My touch is all wrong for iPhones. A friend gave me her old iPhone which was an exercise in complete frustration. An old, basic mobile phone now fails to charge. Will not respond to calls. Hopeless. Accessing a message bank an impossibility. Imagine how spelling abbreviations would screw my already erratic spelling.

'Do not text me, I cannot text.' Friends forget or do not listen. 'I sent you a message,' they complain. My brother sent me a text message for my birthday before Christmas. Exercise in futility. Unknowable is the strength or lack of strength of my fingers. Everyone who can run hands over screens and produce results thinks that everyone else can too. In reality some people cannot.

Disabilities that seem unimaginable to many people are easily ignored.

Dyspraxia

Definition of dyspraxia (DCD)

'Developmental Coordination Disorder(DCD), also known as dyspraxia, is a common disorder affecting fine and/or gross motor coordination in children and adults. This condition is formally recognised by international organisations including the World Health Organization.

An individual's coordination difficulties may affect participation and functioning of everyday life skills in education, work and employment. Children may present with difficulties with self-care, writing, typing, riding a bike, play as well as other educational and recreational activities. In adulthood many of these difficulties will continue, as well as learning new skills at home, in education and work, such as driving a car and DIY.'

(Source: www.bdadyslexia.org.uk/dyslexia/neurodiversity-and-co-occurring-differences/dyspraxia)

CLAIRE MOORE

My Experience of Dyspraxia

Sense of touch faulty
Distances hard to judge
Finger fail with mobile phones
On computer fingers misbehave
Adopt my piano fingering
Unable to ask questions
Words occasionally
hard to pronounce
Falls unending
Family motto
Get up
Get on with it
'Do not cry'
Neck problems
Missed marble step
Spine shred bone
Concussion from falls
Challenging existence
Learning unending.

Claire Moore

Living with Dyslexia and Dyspraxia

Dyspraxia, inherited clumsiness, was the bane of my life. No escape. Molly called me 'Careless Claire'.

'She dropped one of my glass ornaments. It smashed. You have to spank her. She has to be punished.' Molly, who claimed not to believe in corporal punishment, obeyed my aunt's command.

I loved my aunty Doreen, Uncle George's third wife. He was divorced twice. Fred's family are strict Presbyterian. George's divorces were never mentioned. 'So much younger than your uncle. Imagine! He has included Doreen in the act. They stay with us when he is performing in Melbourne. They have the sleep-out off the back verandah.' Doreen never got up before ten o'clock. George left early. Fred did too. I spent a lot of time with *Dordee*. I could not pronounce Doreen. Molly had an Alsatian, Sonia. I called her

So-So. She supplied me with unconditional love and acceptance.

Clock! My first deciphered word. Fred was holding me and I pointed at the clock, establishing great expectations. Under Molly's supervision, Fred built me a swing. Fred or Molly needed to push. Despite lots of instruction, I could not move the swing on my own.

Molly proudly informed people, 'Claire never crawled. She'd tuck her leg under her right hip and stick her left leg out straight while manoeuvring over the floor.' Not realising that not crawling is a precursor to learning difficulties. At 15 months, I could walk, holding onto hands or things but not alone. Drastic action. A specialist prescribed high-backed leather boots. Two pairs. One for daytime, the second for night wear. Molly cut the toes out of the night-time pair.

Being true to my own reality with her was a battle. Molly often would ask me what I wanted and the opposite would occur. Did I want my photograph taken? 'No.' Molly had arranged for a photographer to come and take my photo. Wearing the dreaded brown boots, plus a hand-knitted jumper that Molly had made, which I hated. 'I don't want my photo taken.' A big man with a large black camera was in our lounge room. Molly put a white woollen blanket over a card table in front of curtains. I looked as if

I was sitting on the floor. One of Molly's favourite china dogs was given to me to hold to improve my mood. Holding Loppy did not improve my mood. I did not smile. My photo was taken.

I had a small lump on the middle of my nose. Dr Grieve had a surgery in his home opposite Ascot Vale railway station. Dr Grieve was old. He wore a white coat and glasses. He sat me in the middle of his examination table with my legs dangling over the side. He stuck a small needle in the lump. It disappeared. On the way home in our big black Ford car called Elizabeth, Molly called in at her brothers'. The Wilsons lived at 63 Epsom Road, a single-fronted house on the right side of the block. A large lawn on the second block ran down to a huge privet hedge. Behind the hedge was a two-roomed bungalow. The property ended at a laneway. Uncle Boy drove his car into a shed on the right side of the property. Then came a chook house and a huge vegetable garden. Steep wooden steps led to a back room of their house behind the kitchen. I started to run. Crash! I fell down on my knees, face first. Aunty Glad arrived on the scene, alerted by my wails.

'Stop that now!' Molly commanded.

'That's a bit harsh,' commented Glad.

'I have just had her nose fixed and she falls over on it.'

My knees were always scabbed as were the bottoms of my hands. Molly was not impressed. A daughter always falling over, a clumsy klutz.

Catching balls was always difficult. Impossible to make a top spin. I had a yellow top with a wooden handle that was pumped to make it spin. Laces were impossible for little fingers to tie tight bows. A double bow was an impossibility. Concentrating for long periods of time was a chore.

Aged Three

Father Christmas bought me a peculiar looking bride doll. She had a china head and neck, and partial chest on a cloth body with china arms and legs. Beautiful blue eyes, long dark eyelashes, dark brown hair. I could not manage her hair. Dressed in a white silk bridal gown with a net veil on a silk band, white shoes. Not at all like the one Doreen said I would get when she took me to see Father Christmas in Myers. Being impressed with Princess Margaret, she was named Margaret.

'Why don't you call her Elizabeth? She is much nicer than her sister.'

'She can be Margaret Elizabeth.'

Over time, pressure mounted for a name change.

'I've called her Barbara.'

Molly was not pleased.

Ball and Welch, a department store in Flinders Street, just up from St Paul's Cathedral, sold materials and school uniforms and other things.

'Do you want a new baby?'

'No.'

'Well, I have a baby in my tummy. Do you want a brother or a sister?'

'A sister!'

Molly needed maternity tops so we went on a shopping trip to Melbourne. Walking down Anderson Street to Langs Road to catch the Moonee Ponds red bus to Ascot Vale station where we got off the bus and onto a train. Alighting at Flinders Street station, we walked up a long asphalt ramp to the top. White tiles adorned the walls on the way up. A toilet stop at the Ladies, then off to Ball and Welch where Molly looked at materials and materials and materials. Nothing suited.

'Do you like these, Claire?' I looked, hiding my dismay. Blue cotton material with white spots, pink material with white spots. Medium sized, not too large, not too small. Spots are not my thing. But more shops and searching was too much. Molly made two types in different colours from the same pattern. Oh dear!

In her spare time, Drake was trained to appear at the Royal Melbourne Show. He was my dog. Why couldn't I show him?

'He's much too strong for you to lead. He would pull you over.'

At the Show, I was allowed to sit on a plank stand, provided I did not move or speak to strangers, to watch Molly run round the ring with Mandrake. He got a third place. Bred by Miss Lassal, he was the only dog to be placed. Miss Lassal ignored Drake.

One Sunday morning, Fred and Molly took me and Mandrake to Miss Lassal's place in Toorak Road. Drake met his father, Black Magic, and one of his siblings. An enormous dog fight ensued just as the ladies and gentlemen of Toorak were strolling down Toorak Road to St John's Church. Fred found this was hilarious. Miss Lassal never forgave Mandrake. Although he was an alpha dog, he was attacked by other dogs. Mandrake was my ally and support.

Dogs had to stay overnight at the Showgrounds in the kennels, high off the ground. Fred thought this cruel, so collected Mandrake on his way home from work, thus ending his Show career. Molly was not pleased.

We were at Sorrento, on the beach.

'What have you got, Drake?'

Drake presented Molly with a live chook. Drake has a soft mouth and no killer instinct. Molly removed the chook and returned the shocked fowl to the owner. Molly was mortified.

Fred found a hollowed out loaf of stale white bread on the beach, left for the gulls. He threw the loaf out to sea. Mandrake charged in after the loaf, fetching it. He thought this such a great game. He used to shake salt water droplets all over us when he came out of the sea.

Fred had a toothache. He was in agony. Roots left in his gum after an army dentist extraction. Molly had to drive him to the dentist at Rosebud for an appointment. I was left in a cot in their room at the Sorrento guesthouse. Placed in a cot, I could not escape.

'If you yell, the landlady will come and take you to the toilet.'

I yelled and yelled. No one came. My yells eventually turned into screams. Still no one came. I was so angry. I needed to go to the toilet. I even threw Teddy at my parents' bed. No one came. I pooed my pants. Molly had toilet-trained me by nine months.

MY BUTTERFLY MIND

'Oh, darling.' She picked me up, put me on newspaper and gave me a bath. Fred was minus impacted roots. No one was happy.

Aged Four

It was a very hot February. Molly's baby was overdue by three weeks. 'I do wish this baby would come!'

Angus George Herd was born on the 4th of February 1950 at Jessie McPherson Hospital when the hospital was situated in Williams Street, before shifting adjacent to the Queen Victoria Women's Hospital. He was a big baby. Blond hair and blue eyes. Due to a cold, I was not allowed to visit them in hospital. On the day Fred picked them up, I had to sit in the car and wait for them to arrive. The windows were down. Angus was in a bassinet with handles. Fred drove us home. Uncle George was thrilled to have a nephew. 'He is a champion.' 'The Champ,' George growled. Doreen preferred girls and was not impressed. Fred now had a son and heir. His interaction with his daughter ceased.

Fred was diagnosed with a duodenal ulcer. His doctor gave him a choice. He could give up alcohol or cigarettes. Fred went to work the next day without his cigarette after breakfast. Morning tea, no smoke. Lunch, afternoon tea, the same. After dinner, he was not even tempted when Molly lit her cigarette.

'Claire, your jumping up and down on my stomach caused my ulcer.' Being a literally minded child, I was horrified.

'He's only joking,' Molly claimed.

But I knew he wasn't joking. He would always blame someone else, never himself. Molly had a different theory on the source of the ulcer. Fred had often complained to Molly, 'My mother made me eat a greasy breakfast of bacon and eggs when I had overindulged in drink. She never said a word. Just dished up a completely greasy breakfast when I was too nauseous to eat, but I dutifully ate.'

Molly hated crushing up sulphur tablets to cure my ear abscesses. I hated the stuff mixed with jam or honey. She obviously loved feeding Angus.

'Do you want to go to kindergarten, Claire?'

'No.'

'I don't want you attending Progress Kindergarten. Your aunty Ed is the teacher.'

Yes. And my cousins went there. I would know someone.

I started kindergarten the following week, but not at Progress Kindergarten.

'Why do you love Angus more than me?'

'You refused to breastfeed, that's why.'

Ascot Vale West State School

At five, starting school, for me, was a big adventure. All on my own. Early on Monday morning of my second week at school, the teacher said, 'Your daughter is ambidextrous. She favours her left hand. It being a right-handed world, where even scissors are right-handed, I think she should be made to use her right hand to write.'

'What a good idea. I was left-handed before being made to write with the correct hand. Did me no harm,' Molly claimed.

Writing, for me, became an exhausting chore. My head was so tired, I had to support it with my left hand, my elbow resting on the desk. Writing on a blank page, the letters marched sloping downwards across the page with a mind of their own. Our teacher warned us that reversing certain letters was a symptom of dyslexia. Sometimes I did reverse these letters. I made sure to put them around the right way. Holding my pencil the correct way was impossible for my right hand. I failed to hold my pencil, thumb on the right side, index finger on top with third finger support on the right side. Resting my head on my left hand stopped my head from ending up on the written page. My memory was extraordinary. Memorising stories, poems, songs was easy for me and helped hide any reading problems. Molly would not tolerate any child who did not read.

My knitting style was full of holes. Molly was not impressed. The teacher said, 'She merely needs practice.'

My drawing was not up to standard. It seemed that everything I did was wrong. Boys were lucky. They did not have to knit and escaped to woodwork classes in the old band stand building. Named Old Band Stand Building, originally for band instruments, now used for carpentry. Girls were supposed to knit. I hold the wool the wrong way but it works. Why are they all so fussy?

Grade Four

In the 1950s and '60s, primary school children who were bad spellers or poor readers were regarded by many teachers as dumb. Add poor ability in arithmetic, in particular oral arithmetic, and they were sure you were hopeless. Dyslexia can also disrupt arithmetic, in particular oral arithmetic. By the time the student has worked out what the question means, the way of arriving at the correct answer has slipped away.

In Grade Four, my own battle with arithmetic arrived. Our teacher, Mr Brown, was rotund with white hair and red cheeks. Golden framed spectacles aided his vivid blue eyes. He could have been mistaken for a Father Christmas, minus the beard. Boys who misbehaved were caned on the hand. Appalling behaviour resulted in being sent to sit outside the principal's office for further punishment. Girls were sent out of the class.

Molly claimed not to believe in corporal punishment. She threw it my way three times. Fred would never hit a child. Woe betide anyone who hit his children. His attitude saved both my brother and me from Nan's view, 'Sparing the rod spoilt the child.' Nevertheless, the threat was always there. Molly dished out discipline on the spot.

'I never said to my children, "wait till your father gets home".'

On a bright sunny day with a blue sky beckoning through the high windows, Mr Brown wiped the arithmetic solution off the board. I had already asked him three times how to do these sums. Not game to ask him again, I tried to see how my neighbour did. Mr Brown lost his temper. Dragging me before the whole class, 'Admit you were cheating!' At my silence, he hit me with his huge hands on the top of my arms. This happened three times. After school, I hurried home and Molly showed me how to solve the arithmetic problem. I did not tell her that I had cheated because of the shame and fear of the consequences.

Nature study class the next day. We had to draw the life cycle of the codling moth. I was quite proud of my drawings. Mr Brown made me take my exercise book and walk up and down the aisles, showing everyone the worst drawings in the class. Humiliation unlimited. A cruel man who had to win.

Beginnings

Undiagnosed dyslexia and dyspraxia impacted on my life on separate occasions. While growing up, at times they seemed to intertwine. Being unaware that my periodic spelling mistakes and arithmetic problems were symptoms of dyslexia, I kept trying. Dyspraxia symptoms manifested with balance plus co-ordination problems that resulted in plentiful falls. Molly knew there were problems with my balance and co-ordination. My perceived faults were shameful and humiliating to her. A personal affront that a child of hers could have learning problems. At primary and secondary school, Molly seemed the only one concerned about my ability to learn. Never was the label 'dumb' or 'stupid' applied to me by teachers, cousins or Sunday School teachers. A blessing. Molly's response to me being diagnosed would have been overwhelming.

Molly's siblings, nieces and nephews all seemed to be competing to be the best in Nan's approval. Endless accolades about the joy of competing never stopped. Coming last in races all the time robbed me of any desire to compete.

'Why can't you be more like ...?' a constant refrain from Molly. Fred tried to help in his own way by attempting to teach a toddler to box. How to form a fist to punch, deflect with the other hand. The science of footwork was beyond my comprehension.

Hammers, nails, fingers, a bad combination. My limitations are real. There are ways around most of them. Problems arise to be solved, if not now, eventually there would be a solution. An answer always arrives. Years may pass. I am grateful for minor miracles.

High stress levels encourage my dyslexia and dyspraxia. Haste puts my balance at risk. Astrology claims Sagittarian star sign people are quick on all levels. Physically rushing often leads to calamity for my body. Falling is so easy. I can trip over my own feet, electrical cords, dips in pavements.

'Never look at your feet when walking.' A constant refrain.

'Head up, posture perfect,' intoned Molly. All very well. Impossible when you need to watch your feet to prevent falls. My body's bioreceptors seem to be permanently on strike. Hitting my head when getting into cars. Falling over onto my head. Often resulting in a sore head or concussion. When driving and stopped at red lights, several whiplash incidents resulted in more neck problems. Unending exercise strengthens muscles, ligaments and tendons to take my falls instead of my bones.

Problems of distance lead to problems with perspective. Impossible to draw a crowded skyline correctly. In Grade Six the art teacher informed me that 'You cannot draw.' It took years but I am now able to draw many objects. Not landscapes though.

Dyspraxia presents me with a challenge to stay mobile and free from pain without the use of drugs.

Grade Four, Dyspraxia Manifests

The Band Stand at Ascot Vale West was used as a woodwork room for the boys. The verandah in front of the room was dilapidated, with holes in the flooring. 'Do not run on the Band Stand verandah' was the command. We often sat on the verandah to eat our lunch. Standing up, I slipped over on a banana peel, landing on my left wrist. In class, my desk is in front of Mr Brown's desk.

'Is your arm broken, Claire?'

'The safety officer says it is not.'

The tears are sliding down my face. They will not stop.

'Why are you sobbing?'

'Because it hurts.'

'Is your mother home?'

'No. She's out.'

'Is there anyone's home you can go to?'

'My Nan's.'

Up the lane. All on my own. Dropped my sunglasses and had to pick them up. On tiptoe, I opened Nan's back door.

'What are you doing here, child?'

Nan put me in her bed and massaged my sore wrist.

'Did you know I was once called a very wicked woman?'

'No, Nan.' I could not imagine anyone calling my Nan wicked.

'I was not using my talent for massage. Your great-uncle, Jack, had a cricket injury to his right leg. I found him crawling down the hallway. After my massage, he was right as rain.'

Molly took me to the doctor. My left wrist was fractured.

Ballet lessons were on Sunday, to Molly's chagrin. She wanted us to do family things together on Sundays. Practising the Highland Fling in Molly's kitchen, I slipped, landing on my right hand. Another fracture.

'You slipped on some fat on the kitchen floor,' Molly said. Strange, Molly never let any mark, let alone fat, linger on her kitchen floor. Molly made a tutu for me to wear at our ballet concert. The Skaters Waltz was the highlight of the ballet concert. Or would have been if I had remembered to put the hat on the snowman. End of ballet career.

Molly's elder sister, Edna, married Douglas Munro. They had one daughter, Grace. The family lived with Nan and Pop. Uncle Doug's father, Skip, died. On the day of the funeral, 'Claire, you are to wait for your elder cousins. Walk to Nan's up the lane with them.'

Uncle Boy had two sons, younger than me. We got out early.

'Come on, Claire. Come up with us.'

'No. Molly said to wait.'

The older cousins laughed at me and ran away. My legs hurt and my lungs felt like they would burst. I ran as fast as I could.

Nan.

'Why are you so late, child? You were meant to be early.' Nobody said a word. I slipped into the only vacant chair.

Pop said he would teach me chess. He never did. Pop's shed squatted between the stable and the toilet, accessed via Nan's huge laundry. In Pop's shed one could only see layers of dirt on the floor.

An old tree stump, used as a block to chop wood, resided under the swing. The swing seat was made of wood; strong ropes fastened the swing to a beam. Sitting on the swing, talking to Pop.

'You are such a chatterbox,' he complained. Bang! Falling backwards. Hitting my head on the chopping block edge. Tears spring unchecked from my eyes.

'Don't cry. It doesn't hurt.'

'Hurt! It hurt!'

Pop lost me. Could not stand my tears. Failed to understand my reality. In the bathroom, Doug and Molly thrust my head down into the basin, between the cups Nan and Pop used for their false teeth. Doug poured Dettol on my wound. Boy, did it sting! Molly took me to the doctor who covered the small hole in my head with wax.

'Such a clumsy child. So careless.'

Poppy made me a doll's pram, table and a chair for my dolls. Molly claimed, 'Not for you, Claire. He made them for me.'

Molly had a set of commandments that applied only to me! Never to other children. Bitten by a friend, in front of Molly, there were no consequences. A classmate hit me with a fence paling, the mother agreed that we should play at her place after school. Long walking distances for me, to and fro. She never came to mine. Girls of whom Molly disapproved were speedily routed.

'You love your cousins,' Molly was forever telling me, leaving me puzzled.

On the afternoon Pop died, Molly left us with the plumber who stayed till Fred arrived home. We sat at the dining room table eating dinner. Molly arrived.

'Pop died,' she said. I burst into tears.

'Tears are so selfish. You are crying because you miss Pop. You are not crying for him.'

Never did I see Molly cry.

Grade Five, Ascot Vale West School

In the original red brick school building, Grade Five was up on the first floor. The teacher sat on her chair in front of her table on a slightly raised wooden platform, in front of a large green blackboard. She had us all sitting in order of her perception of our academic ability. This resulted in the boy who needed the most scholastic help banished to the last desk on the left side of the class. Two desks behind me, an Italian girl of 13 was isolated while she waited to turn 14 to become a factory worker. Nobody ever spoke to her.

One bright sunny day, the principal, Mr Vizard, descended upon us. Our task before recess was to copy the text on the board into our writing exercise books.

'At the end of the lesson, your teacher will collect all your books for me to inspect. There will be no mistakes.'

On the right-hand side of each of our desks was a small round hole containing a white china inkwell full of blue ink. Armed with a nib affixed to a slim wooden holder as a pen, trying my best, I dipped my pen into the inkwell. Splash! A huge blue ink blob spread over the top of my page, and it was not possible to rip out the page and start again. Before our break, back came Mr Vizard.

'Whose book is this? The worst page in the class!'

I put up my hand. Disaster! Molly never knew. Shame and humiliation were often my companions. My parents disapproved of poor marks. Mistakes were constant, but I always passed. Fred's ire at my lack of sporting ability was an ever-present elephant that I ignored most of the time. Molly covered up a lot of my disabilities from Fred, who was not interested anyway.

'Why can't you top the class like your brother?'

Angus claimed he had never topped the class. He did receive a Commonwealth Scholarship for university. Very clever.

In classes with 40 to 45 students at primary school, no teacher had the time needed to devote to problem students. Individual tuition a pipedream. The problems of dyslexia were well known by my first primary school teacher. Many dyslexic and dyspraxic students fell through the cracks without diagnosis. Shame and humiliation are experienced because you are not equipped to read or perform sport like so-called 'normal' children. Children become adept at hiding their disabilities from others. Early diagnosis is essential for the development of these children's potential.

Nan

Molly's mother, known as Nan, was a professional pianist. On an assignment in New Zealand, she met Charles Wilson and married him, thus ending her professional music career. She channelled her musical talents into playing church organs, alternating between Anglican and Presbyterian churches. Her focus within the family was on producing a male child. Fred came from a Scots family who believed 'All wealth should be left to the eldest son.' As he was the fifth son and the seventh child, his attitude puzzled me. As a girl, neither family approved of me so I began a battle for fairness and equality that obscured other issues. I was six when at Nan's on my own after school. Molly did not want me to learn the piano, nor did I.

'You want to learn the piano, Claire, don't you?'

'Yes.'

'Come on, child. I'll give you your first lesson.'

Thus began my first piano lesson. On the way out, the razor straps glared from the towel rails in the bathroom, opposite the piano room.

'If you don't behave, they'll be around your legs, child. Molly, I have just given Claire her first piano lesson. The lessons are free but you will have to pay for the music required.' Checkmate, Nan. Nan would schedule piano lessons at the same time as my cousin Helen's. Sometimes we raced down Charles Street to Nan's. I was always last. An hour's wait, sitting still on a chair outside Nan's piano room. The only time I won, Nan was out so Helen gave me a lesson in 'Chopsticks', 'Blue Moon', 'Can You Wash Your Father's Shirt?' We were having a great time when Nan walked in.

'Out!' Punishment was to be dispensed.

Suddenly, the door slammed. Molly walked into the dining room.

'There you are, Claire. I was so worried when you failed to arrive home on time.' Nan said not a word. We all walked home together, saved from the storm.

Mozart's music, when played softly, is reputed to encourage both sides of the brain to communicate. An hour's piano practice daily, unbeknown to me, was increasing my spelling ability. My cousin Grace was not so lucky. She lived with her parents and

Nan. Who still lived by the motto, 'Spare the rod and spoil the child.'

Left in Pop's care for the afternoon, while he was busy in his shed creating something, forgetting all about us, we decided to play shop. We had a long stool as a counter with nothing to sell. So we went for a stroll down Charles Street, almost to Epsom Road, in the days when flowering gums formed a barrier between footpath and road. On our journey, we collected empty cigarette packets for our store. We piled them up on our bench as we were ready to open our stall. The wire door opened. Out stepped Nan, a grim expression on her face.

'What are you doing?'

'Playing shop.'

'Where did you get this rubbish?'

'From the street.'

'Home you go,' she said to me, leaving poor Grace to face a belting with a hairbrush. Molly's abuse was mainly verbal.

Penleigh

Classes in secondary school were held in the relatively new brick buildings next to the original old house. Next-door neighbours were not always friendly or tolerant of the school. In Forms One and Two, our classroom rear wall consisted of wooden doors that folded back, exposing the view of the basketball court. This let cool air circulate on hot days. The class windows facing the fence were too high to see out when sitting down. When on the war path, the middle-aged lady next door would stand on the fence, rising like a furious puppet. A white head would appear over the fence line. Harsh words would be hurled at our fascinated faces. Our teachers would depart to inform the headmistress. We could then express our amusement. Poor lady! We fed her chooks all sorts of things through small holes in the fence. The chooks even consumed sandwich paper. Not good for their digestion. Lectures were delivered on not feeding the chooks at all. Life would quieten down until the next episode. Later her children were forbidden to sell her land to the school.

Our English lesson was enlivened when the teacher asked us, 'What does the word compost mean?' My hand shot up with the correct answer.

'How did you know that?' she enquired. Never were other students asked how they knew something. She'd asked us this question a month before. I had answered correctly when others in the class failed to remember. Boredom with lessons repeated, or uninteresting, resulted in gazing at the sky outside, counting or creating images in my head.

The maths teacher had a temper, regularly losing her cool with us. She would then storm off demanding an apology, refusing to return unless we apologised. She could be played by the more adventurous in the class. Impossible to catch up in maths, she consigned all girls who were only interested in arithmetic to seats on the far left in a line of desks from front to the back. Another girl and I shared the back desks as we did not need her help. In Grade Six, a teacher gave us mental arithmetic, making the individual stand up till she solved the problems. My arithmetic improved immensely under her tutelage.

History was my favourite subject. No notes! How wonderful! We underlined the essential points to learn in our textbooks. No lines to write, or reams of notes, which was so exhausting for me to achieve. Free from the drudge of writing, I could concentrate on facts. Alone in not wanting to write notes while most of the class were unimpressed with no notes. The freedom from notes encouraged my passion for history and later the writing of family histories.

Marvellous Meg, our biology and domestic science teacher, sacrificed many lunch hours helping me and another student with our spelling. Meg had faith in my abilities. The arts teacher was brilliant with art and needlework. My inability with space in drawing was an insurmountable problem. She acknowledged that I had a great sense of colour. Unfortunately, she had no control over the class. In Form One, two of the tougher girls in the class had a fist fight in front of her desk.

'Girls, girls. Stop!' she exclaimed, wringing her hands before leaving to find help. Molly handled all my sewing homework on her unusable treadle machine for me. She made so many mistakes in the work, I almost failed.

'Well, you would have made mistakes.' A classmate's mother made no mistakes when machining for her daughter. My final year decorative needlework saved the day. No machines needed. My marks were good.

In my final year, our geography teacher told the class she was passing out a test result in mark order.

Feeling pleased as the test had seemed easy, she called out all the others' marks. My heart was in my shoes.

'Claire, you have topped the class.' Relief.

The female singing teacher despaired of our class and the one below us. The principal used to stroll into our singing classes to make sure we were singing, not just mouthing the words.

In second form, we painted our classroom. The Parents' Association paid for the paint. Molly was the only parent who accepted the invitation to help us paint. Molly was a proficient painter of walls, etc. We were so proud of our achievement. No doubt modern scholars would not be allowed to paint their classroom.

Our final year English teacher was notable for an expressionless face. She refused to smile or frown because to do so would cause wrinkles on her face. What an amazing amount of energy she expended. She never commented on my spelling.

Boater straw hats were worn in summer, berets in winter with seamed stockings. Keeping the seams straight was an unending task. Gloves worn, not to be lost. Not an easy thing to achieve. In my last year, my cousin's old summer uniforms saved Molly money.

Our Black Watch tartan pinafores were allowed to be cut down to skirts.

In Form Four Penleigh, an amazing trip was planned for the girls in our grade to Central Australia. I so wanted to go. All the class signed up for the trip.

'What? You prefer to go away with your classmates instead of coming to New Zealand with me to meet Pop's relatives?' Molly claimed she paid for the trip. Fred said, 'It nearly broke me.'

In Christchurch, climbing alone all the way up a narrow circular stone stairway to the belfry steps in the Anglican Cathedral, terror arrived. Fear of falling from one of several steps past the bells, nothing to hold to prevent a fall, in order to take in the view from the spire balcony. Turning back was not an option. Molly expected an account of the view. An amazing view. A wonderful city with parks and a magic river spread out before me. Getting down, another challenge, my knees nearly collapsed on arriving at street level. Mrs Giddley and Molly each took an arm till my walking returned to normal.

Windy Wellington and Molly's cousins. Molly wrote in her diary that 'Claire got on well with her cousins.' Nan's family, not Pop's. In Waitara, the cousins were on Pop's side. All older than me, the second cousins mostly younger. Elsie with the smiling face, Molly's cousin, corresponded with me. Strong determined women a feature of the family. My lack of self-esteem was meant to be fixed by the New Zealand trips. Molly was bitterly disappointed.

Never again did I feel part of my class.

Sport

Ascot Vale West Primary School favoured male sports, both football (Australian Rules) and cricket played in a huge grassed area in the rear of the school, ending at the laneway. The caretaker's house faced Victory Parade. On sports days, girls were confined to an asphalt square to play basketball or rounders. No one bothered much about their games or sporting abilities.

Penleigh took sport very seriously. The girls divided among three houses: Chaucer — red, Dorset — blue, and Park — green. Marian, my oldest female cousin, gained a half and full blue for sport. Helen, her sister, and Grace, our cousin, were all in Chaucer. Poor Chaucer gained me as a member, three years behind my nearest cousins. Second goalie in the second basketball team kept me out of the intense bustle of the basketball court. Baseball was a different matter. No one wanted to pick me in their team. Our sports mistress forced my selection in a side every week, usually out after three strikes. Occasionally ball and bat connected. Bang! Off flew the ball. Crash! The bat landed, thrown backwards, making the girls behind me jump away. Sometimes, despite my poor running ability, I arrived at first base. Over five years, three or four home runs were achieved, with lots of encouragement from the team! Learning hockey occurred in our back paddock. Instinctively, I knew never to try.

Every year the school held running races for the houses at a local park further down the street and across the road from the school. All secondary children were expected to participate in the competition, so vital to their development. Such fun for the winners. No fun for me. My right ankle would twist. Over I'd fall. Get up, get on, run last. Poor runners were forced into the cross ball teams and the tunnel ball teams. The easy sports. Unfortunately, not easy for me. The winners represented our house in the annual sporting games held at the old Essendon football ground, known as Windy Hill. On my first sports day, I tried too hard. Dropped the cross ball. The tunnel ball went *whoosh* through my legs. Fred, disgusted by my performance, never attended another sports event. Worse, Fred had me taught swimming by the best, Mr Joe O'Brien, at the Melbourne City Baths. He knew I could swim. My backstroke was quite good. I hated swimming with others splashing around me, so even when chosen, I always escaped the event. When

I was 17 he said, 'You never tried, did you?' I burst into tears, a complete failure. 'You bloody little psychopath.' He never knew how hard I had tried.

Tennis, I knew all the rules, could serve the occasional ace. At least the ball usually flew over the net. A social game ended by dyspraxic falls.

Cricket was an essential skill because my brother needed more than Molly and Fred to play backyard cricket. Totally unable to bowl over arm, my underarm grubbers gained many wickets. When the ball sailed over the back fence, you were in for nought or out for six. At family picnics, my fielding position was way out in the outfield, away from any action. My failure to catch balls was infamous.

Dyspraxia Strikes

Penleigh. A bright sunny day. Physical Education class in your newly refurbished hall, paid for by government donations for the first time. 'I pay to send you to school. Why should government taxes be involved?' Sunshine enlivened the obstacles awaiting us. Up a thick rope, each of us had to climb up without burning hands on the way down. Then race to a form, lying upside down, and walk quickly along the narrow supporting beam. Jump down, turn right, run across a mat, jump up onto a wooden horse, somersault off, forward roll. My neck and body moved to the right causing three neck vertebrae to jam against my skull as I fell off the horse. No one caught me!

'An X-ray may reveal nothing. It costs money,' intoned the orthopaedic surgeon.

'Take it anyway,' Molly replied.

'Well, you were right. Six weeks off school.'

A surgical collar. Visits to the doctor three times a week for manipulation. October tests performed at home, Molly supervised. Up for an hour, two in bed. Molly resented having to take me to the doctor. His manipulations helped straighten my neck. Physical Education classes ceased. Two study periods instead.

At the beginning of the following year, the school photographer wanted to exclude me from our class photograph. My appearance, sporting a dark green scarf over my plastic neck brace, quite ruined his photo. The form mistress informed him that excluding me meant no photograph. Eventually, I was seated in the middle of the front row, holding the class identification. Visible differences unacceptable to many people.

Undiagnosed Dyspraxia

During my final year at school, Fred had to drive me to Charles Street to catch the school bus. Then pick me up at four o'clock. Molly had to drive me to and from our GP. Nan was ill again. She had another heart attack. Heart attacks seemed frequent especially if Nan was not getting her own way. This time her dormant rodent ulcer had flared up again. Medical advice of a cure was false. Jean and Molly nursed her in shifts at night. Ed had the daytime shifts. Nan wished to die at home. Her daughters were defeated in this by gangrene arriving in both of Nan's feet. Lying in her double bed made it impossible for her girls to turn their mother. Hospital became the only option. Luckily, Nan had been made a life governor of the Queen Victoria Hospital for all her fundraising activities. A bed was available for her in a private room. There was a new modern mattress for her. At 5.30 on a Wednesday morning, the phone rang. Lying in bed in my high ceilinged brown room, I did not have to be told Nan was dead. Right in the middle of my final exams. British History. I was good at that. After the exam I wanted to talk about Nan. No one would listen. The pain of loss had to be expressed, tears flowed. My history teacher arrived.

'Nan's dead.'

'Your mother phoned the school and asked them not to talk about it.'

Biology examination was next, after lunch. Half the paper I did not know. Our teacher had told us the exam was a punt because it was impossible to teach all the syllabus. Waiting for the paper results, a tense time, I failed English and Biology. Fred expected me to go to commercial college and embark on a career as a legal secretary. He refused to pay for my final year at Penleigh. Molly paid for my final term as a one off. So unfair. No more school for me.

Leaving school in a mini recession. Molly dragged me around town, forcing me to go into businesses to enquire if they had any positions available for someone like me. Humiliation at the weather bureau when told, 'You need a university degree to work here.'

After working as junior clerk at Prahran Hodges, mastering a cord switchboard, learning to type at night school, I sailed through Leaving English attending Taylor's Business College at night school. They were so clear about what was expected. Passing

English was not a problem. Once the challenge of a job faded, it was time for me to move on.

There is no concept for me of my body in space. Elbows repeatedly knock things off shelves, feet trip over extension leads or any little thing. No co-ordination. Poor balance. Small hands, small feet. Weak ankles and weak wrists all contributed to mishaps. Nobody took any notice of a clumsy klutz.

Denial of Dyslexia

The clues of dyslexic symptoms were there for years. Constant dealing with stress from verbal abuse. Many times my thoughts were kept to myself to avoid remarks that Fred or my brother would consider stupid. Shock at verbal attacks often keeps me silent. Awe at other students' ability to promote themselves silenced and defeated me.

In my final year at school, after an absence from school, I was thrust into a group of fellow students who professed a desire to become teachers. Deposited at Teachers' College, we were shown into a classroom, seated in a circle on chairs and each girl waxed lyrical on why they wanted to become teachers. Shamed by their ability, silence descended upon me.

Not a word could I say as to why a teaching career would be ideal for me. I felt humiliated by the end of my teaching career before it had begun. After leaving school, not even kindergartens were interested in my services.

Lesson: always try. Others' successes, combined with an awareness of their abilities, revealed my spasmodic performance in my class, further lowering my low self-esteem. It has taken me years to realise that shock is part of my dyslexia and dyspraxia. Stress levels increased a great deal with external exams. Luckily we sat for the exams at school. In Form Four our intermediate German exams required an oral reciting of a poem at the Goethe Society, a German speaking society. My hands shook, my voice shook. The judges were kind. Unfortunately, that year too many students passed German. The pass mark was raised to 53. My mark, 50. So infuriating for me. If not enough students passed a subject, the official pass mark would be lowered. Stress exacerbated all my symptoms of dyslexia.

Compared to my first year at school, studying English at night school with Taylor's Business College was so easy! Typed manuals of all exercises and course requirements. An external exam at the end of the year at the Exhibition Building, a foreign environment for me, in a huge hall. Rows and rows of single desks with solitary chairs in long lines, we were allowed pens, pencils and rulers. The English exam was so easy that I finished early and had time to re-read my answers. My focus on answering the question asked correctly paid off. Lower stress levels helped me to pass.

All Saints Church, Ascot Vale

Family church, for Molly, her younger sister Jean, and their families. At Sunday School we learnt stories from the Bible, about all sorts of characters, Abraham, Sarah, Rachael, Joseph and his coat of many colours, Joshua and the battle of Jericho, Naomi and Ruth, the creation story, Adam and Eve. Eve was blamed for Adam's sin. No responsibility for men? Only men spoke in church, moral stories as examples of the behaviour required of children as Christians. Christmas and Easter stories central to our faith. I did well at Sunday School. No exams, ergo no nerves. Attendance records were important. Prizes were given for attendance or work well done. Prayers and hymns were taught. I loved the hymns and singing. I loved stained glass windows. Our religious education was presented as the one truth. Missionaries were admired.

At an early age, when standing at the back of the church waiting to be admitted in the middle of the service, I observed that every important task was done by men. There was no room for women in the church. On the way to church, at times, we heard Ian Ames playing upon the piano.

'Why can't you play like him?' Molly was fond of asking.

For years we had our roast dinners on Saturday night. The purchase of a washing machine changed everything on Sunday. Molly was asked and decided to teach Sunday School. A pianist for the Sunday School had arrived.

Fred rescued the clean wash from the new washing machine and pegged out the wash on the clothesline, in between preparing and putting a roast dinner in the oven, timed for our return from church.

Molly enjoyed teaching Sunday School. She focused more on Jesus' spirituality as in the St James version of the Bible than church doctrine. I was teaching Sunday School, as was an elder cousin. All the young teachers attended one of Billy Graham's Crusades at the Melbourne Cricket Ground. Molly was bombarded from many sides with the instruction, 'You must be born again.' Molly was unimpressed.

I was allowed to sing at Sunday School anniversaries. Singing a duet with another girl, I sang flat, so all singing lessons were stopped. Fred slept through the whole performance. The choir walked out after the minister and there was Fred, sound asleep in the back row.

Suddenly, Angus did not have to attend Sunday School anymore. Molly refused to say why. Years later, I discovered he had followed in Fred's footsteps. He wagged Sunday School and spent his collection money. Molly kept secrets from me.

Sunday School Picnics

Lunches packed with soft drink bottles, arriving at the church between 9.30 am and 10.00 am, excited children with their Sunday School teachers waited for the furniture van to arrive. Wooden, freestanding benches ran across the sides of the van and shorter ones across the middle space, in rows. Teachers, adults on the side forms, excited children crammed in the middle forms. No windows. The trip from Ascot Vale to Eltham Park was a great adventure. Not many people had cars. No one had ever heard of seatbelts. We all sang songs on the trip out. An example was *'Ten green bottles hanging on the wall. If one green bottle should accidentally fall, there would be nine green bottles hanging on the wall.'* Nursery rhymes were allowed. Hymns did not feature. We were almost free.

Upon arrival, we herded out of the van. The church elders had set up an area for games. An egg and spoon race. Great if the eggs are hard boiled. Calamity if they are not. Bad enough egg and spoon races, but sack races. Really! Designed to make me fall over. The adults and more competitive among us thought this was such fun. Worse was to come with the two-legged race. Being a fool in front of everyone is not my idea of fun. After eating our lunch, we all walked around the lake. Suddenly it was time for us to pile into the furniture van again and head off to Ascot Vale, where we were met by parents or older siblings and escorted home.

Holy Trinity Anglican Church

Upon being uprooted from All Saints Anglican Church in Ascot Vale West, we became part of the congregation at Holy Trinity. At least, Molly and I did. Angus was not forced to attend church. Molly never said why. Teaching Sunday School at Ascot Vale had been interesting, stimulating. Molly taught. Marian, one of my cousins, taught. Aunty Jean did the church flowers. Molly often supplied the flowers, she played hymns on the piano for the Sunday School children, we formed part of the church community. In Newmarket, the local church was cold, unwelcoming. Teaching a preschool Sunday class was fun. Kensington parish was a very poor parish. The children in my class were immaculately dressed in their best clothes every Sunday. Our vicar was new to the parish, young and single.

'I have no luck with youth groups,' he complained to me. No wonder! The diocese decreed that pennies and threepences (worth three pennies) were not enough for the collection box. Sixpences and shillings were to be given. The hymn 'All Things Bright and Beautiful' was to be prohibited, not because of equality issues but because of the verse, 'If we have no money, we can give him love. He'll accept our offering, smiling from above.' When no offering was forthcoming, the children were validated with the song being sung as the collection was taken up. The church demanded more money. The vicar told me to visit the parents of my Sunday School class to discover why they did not attend church.

I visited two families. A mother opened the door to me. Bare floorboards. Seven single beds in the lounge, all piled high with unironed clothes. Who was the more embarrassed? The mother or me?

Visiting the high rise flats in Debney's Paddock provided wonderful views. Lack of money prevented the residents' church attendance. The vicar needed to do his job and visit the parents. It was not mine.

The Anglican church provided books with lessons for each Sunday, controlling the content of lessons in line with church doctrine. Two nights a week I had night school. A third night out at the vicarage was too much. I had issues with doctrine over Jesus stories, so I resigned.

Words as Symbols

Words sting, lash, discourage, shut down, labelled when you cannot. Careless when trying hard. 'Stupid' label discourages. 'Try harder.' You are trying hard. No way can you try harder. 'Pay attention.' Words missed, changed instructions. You think you have completed the task. The task you had was different.

'Why did you not pay attention? Idiot.'

'The dictation is easy.'

'Not to me it's not. No words to tell.'

'You don't listen to me.'

'I do.'

A dyslexic child in a family of perfect spellers. Parental expectations high.

'Why can't you be like the others? You need to concentrate more.'

I concentrate but I am still called stupid. My parents are angry at my school results.

'No one cares. I hate you! You always tell me how stupid I am!' Tears.

'You would if you could, but you cannot, so you won't.' An imagined conversation between a dyslexic child and adults. Such children often cannot decode symbols visually, may be unable to hear all oral instructions because of not being able to distinguish the correct oral symbols to respond. Adults' body language often scares children who are different. Frowns, mouth turned down in disapproval, expressions of intolerance, frustration. Subtle symbols effective as the spoken word in demolishing a child's self-esteem. Words become mines of the mind.

Instead, it may be more effective to encourage a child to explore interests, or ways that work for that individual child. So many parents of dyslexic children seem to focus on the negatives, ignoring their strengths. Being the butt of jokes creates more sadness. Anger becomes a great mask for anguish. Parents and teachers need to be aware of body language and how damaging it can be to children who cannot understand. Mouths turned down in disapproval, frustration, intolerance, frowns in anger, increasing the volume of one's voice. These children generally hear well. Hands across chest, glares, subtle signs that cause damage, more effective than the spoken word, becoming a weapon that lowers self-esteem. Such actions can be unconscious. At times, the adult is fully aware of the consequences of their actions.

Ways of sharing information. Words are written symbols. Speech is spoken symbols. That can be broken into syllables. Phonics aid dyslexics who can understand them.

Trying to decode Indigenous names from stick drawings of people with labels in an Indigenous language gave no clues to pronunciation. Indigenous painters create symbols with dot paintings. Dot paintings tell stories. Some I may decipher, not others. Indigenous people must decode their own language symbols, dot painting, together with English language symbols. A huge task. Harder still if an indigenous child has the added burden of dyslexia.

Dyslexia, for me, means the frustration of often forgetting other people's names, such as the name of a lifelong friend, not being able to introduce her. Short courses in remembering names failed. Most people remember my name, amplifying the problem. Life is spent decoding different symbols. Sight creates images in my mind. Hearing is essential to my spelling. Words to spell eventuate from phonics. At times, I can look straight at an object that my eyes fail to see.

Being able to correctly decipher words to read and write are accomplishments required by all children. Becoming aware of the intense pressure to excel, not just to perform, on an acceptable level can lead to many dyslexic children concealing what they see as their inadequacies. Shamed by both guilt and the humiliation of never being acceptable, or good enough, eats away at self-esteem. Ridicule further decreases self-esteem. Fear of being discovered never bothered me because I never knew I was dyslexic. I could read, my focus distracted by other issues.

Comparison between children who are literate and those not literate in a family further erodes self-esteem. 'You are not trying,' both parents and teachers admonish. They do not know how hard you are struggling. Feelings of rage at not succeeding are either acted out or suppressed. Many dyslexic individuals conceal their problems. Leaving school early, overwhelmed by what they perceive as their failure and inadequacies. All people are equal, except when you cannot decipher symbols, when you fail to recognise common symbols. Then it becomes easier to be excluded from mainstream learning. Unlike a broken leg, dyslexia and dyspraxia are invisible challenges. Embarking on the challenge of discovering how a child learns requires patience, persistence and faith. Families need to work together. Differing styles of learning need to be explored and accepted by schools. One size does not suit all. Competition seems to be encouraged between siblings and students at the expense of co-operation. For instance a dyslexic girl was constantly compared to her two literate brothers. She could draw simultaneously with both hands. A triumph. Her brothers could not. The mother refused to explore her daughter's abilities. Understanding and a willingness to explore other options were dismissed.

Language

Molly as an elocutionist insisted on me speaking correctly. Sounding all vowels and relevant consonants was important to her. Dropping an 'h' or a 'g' was almost a cardinal sin. By emphasising correct pronunciation when conversing with me and while reading to me, my ears picked up sounds while my mind formed pictures and words. Molly was teaching me the sounds or phonics. Phonics are often sounds of each letter in a word. Vowels are control letters in words. There are long vowels as in 'ape'. The long vowel is identical with the vowel letter. Short vowels as in 'hat'. Short vowels, at times, have only one vowel. Extensive information on vowels and syllables can be found in Elsie Smelt's book *A Complete Guide to English Spelling*. Hearing sounds gives a clue as to how to spell words correctly. Stress is a factor in my erratic spelling. Perhaps my mind runs ahead of the letters, while my ears, at times, hear the wrong letters. Such as 'new' instead of 'knew'. The list of words is endless.

A mind that sees completed sentences on a page, when the last words are lost, produces dangling sentences. Dangling sentences only became apparent in my leaving examinations. They keep recurring.

Appreciating the Music of Words

Music is based on sounds and vibrations, particularly if playing by ear, where you rely totally on the ear to create tunes. Reading music can be relied on to play the piano. Sight playing involves reading musical notes. My style in piano playing is to read the notes from sheet music and listen to the sounds created upon the keyboard.

Some teachers, and modalities such as kinesiology, as noted previously, believe that dyslexia is caused by the left side of the brain and the right side of the brain failing to communicate. This theory makes sense to me.

At primary school, from ages six to twelve, piano practice took over an hour of my time every day. My spelling was OK until piano practice ceased. Completely unaware of any other benefit from my piano practice at that time. Another advantage was my familiarisation with works of classical significance, Beethoven's music was masterly in expressing emotions without words. Helped me to become aware of my own suppressed emotions. In music, the beat, tone, pitch, tempo are all important as an aid to my hearing.

Speeches, reciting a poem, reading a play aloud can produce the same sounds in my ears by tone, pitch, beat and harmony. Thus speech and oral performance hold musical qualities for me that helped me learn to read while giving me much enjoyment. Molly always sang and encouraged singing. Listening to songs to learn a tune, singing involved reading then remembering words. All this aided my learning to understand sounds for reading.

Other Languages

Languages other than English are incomprehensible to me. Hearing and reading are different kinds of challenges. German, for me, is a similar language to English. I could just cope. Pronunciation in French and German was not a problem. Our language teacher was French and indoctrinated us with a Parisian French accent. Her German accent was also excellent. My ears could easily follow. I was not afraid of pronunciation in those languages. However, Italian vowels, to me, are incomprehensible. I learnt 'please', 'thank you', 'buongiorno', etc. Nearly fainted when an Italian complimented me on my Italian! Much too embarrassed to practise pronunciation in Italian. Chinese is a tonal spoken language. My ears fail to distinguish the correct sounds. I was helping a Chinese student to learn English. She attempted to teach me Chinese. That did not work out well.

My limited Italian greetings, I now realise, were often expressed in cafes in Lygon Street and other Italian restaurants, when staff greeted customers in Italian. Probably on a subconscious level, I must have picked up some pronunciation skill. Imitating is easier than spelling for me.

No use to tell me I can learn another language. I would if I could, but I cannot so I won't. Written words in French and German were easier. I actually enjoyed working out what the texts meant. I think interpreters and others who are multilingual are amazing.

Indigenous paintings, to me, are wonderful. Maybe it's the symbolism and the colours and shapes. On the other hand, correct or any pronunciation of country names is impossible for me. Looking at pictures with labels in dialect does my head in. How clever are they to speak English and their own languages. Being dyslexic would make life in the cities impossibly hard.

And then shorthand was a completely different concept which was so hard for me. A whole term of night school, two hours a week, wasted on shorthand. What a joke. Still, some squiggles stuck in my mind. Fred's Hansard earned him awards. He was aware of my spelling inadequacies. Reading Shakespeare's plays and sonnets, Chaucer and his *Canterbury Tales*, all helped my reading and improved my writing. Music has been a great aid to me, but may not always help others in the same manner.

I am an educational challenge, but a very experienced problem solver.

Pianos and Other Matters

'Claire, I am going to leave the Herd piano to Kate, my first grandchild. You don't mind, do you?'

'No.' What else could I say. Previously the piano was to be mine.

'You'll never guess what happened on Monday.'

'What happened on Monday?'

'Go into the lounge and look behind the door.'

'Why? What happened to the piano?'

'Jo sent a van to collect it.'

Molly was mortified. She was now without a piano.

'It was to go to Kate after my death. Not to Jo this week.'

Originally the piano belonged to Olive Herd, Fred's second sister. After she married, the beautiful piano stayed at 24 McCracken Street, Kensington. When Olive died, her five-year-old daughter shared a room with Annie, our grandmother. She married, moved away and the piano remained. My room in Ascot Vale never felt like mine. In old age, Annie lived with my parents. Molly had to nurse a bedridden Annie through kidney failure. She was terrified of both birth and death, yet she helped to lay out Annie in her room after she died. Annie's room, not mine. A discovery I made many years later.

When Annie moved in with Fred and Molly, her companions rented the McCracken Street house. The house was single-fronted with very steep steps up to the front door. Down the hall, into the lounge room where the Herd piano sat deserted and neglected next to the left wall. Drawn blinds prevented any light from daring to enter. After auctioning McCracken Street, the Herd piano took pride of place in our lounge room. Rejuvenated by my daily piano practice, Molly used the piano when teaching some of Angus's classmates to play the recorder. She played nursery rhymes, carols, hymns and classical pieces plus all types of songs.

When I was 12, Nan stated:

'When I was your age, I practised on the piano for four hours a day.' Well, that sunk me. I was struggling to play for one hour a day, with no desire to practise for four hours a day. That was the end of my piano lessons. In retrospect, my spelling deteriorated in secondary school. Somehow the piano playing and music had helped.

At secondary school, my homework load increased. Fred spent Saturdays watching local football. Escaping the house to join Fred, imagining that we were sharing an experience, sitting in our car in the front seat, watching the football and studying. In the morning, Ascot Vale Youth Centre under 17 team played at Walter Street Reserve. The cars drove onto the reserve and parked at the street end of the oval. Fred would walk around the field, practising what he called psychological warfare. 'Drop the ball, let it go,' he'd yell. A lot of the opposing team players fell for this tactic, perhaps because they were young. Home for lunch. Off to Fairburn Park, where a further two Ascot Vale teams played. Doug Munro, our uncle, coached all three teams. He was still playing football at 40. The teams played in the Essendon District Football League. Essendon was our local VFL team and very much part of the community. Molly purchased membership tickets for herself and me, embarking on an interest as an Essendon fan. On an empty field, Fred would punch a football at me. If no one was in the goal square, he taught me to kick a punt and drop kick through the goals.

The Herd piano accompanied us to Newmarket. Sailed around the corner to Westbourne Road when the mansion was demolished to make way for new loading races that removed the cattle from the streets. Continued on to Oak Park before finally returning to Ascot Vale. Our piano always settled in front of an internal wall to preserve tone and tuning. Whipped away to a new home in Kangaroo Ground where Kate's mother held Christmas Eve carol parties, left behind when their relationship ended. Married 40 years, Fred took Molly into Allans Music store in Collins Street and purchased her a piano. 'He did not quibble at the price.' Molly was so happy. Two months later, she dies at home, six days before Christmas. Molly's possessions left to me to stay at Fred's, until he was ready to let them go. Loading the piano and paintings onto the back of a rental van.

'What are you doing with that piano? It belongs to Mr Herd. Are you stealing it?'

'No. It was my mother's, now mine. We are taking it home.'

'Alright then.' The concerned neighbour walked away.

Binoculars and Other Matters

Fred and Molly loved horses, especially racehorses. Fred would give Molly a five shilling stake to be placed with the local SP bookie. Molly would back doubles with a payout of 80 pounds or more. She would always give Fred his stake money back. He did not care. Backing winners impossible for me, let alone a double. Molly was lucky. She hit a hole in one at the old Rosebud golf course. Fred never did. When watching from the stands at a racecourse, binoculars are important for punters to view the field on the course opposite. Fred often gave me binoculars so I could enjoy the sight.

Impossible for me to focus binoculars to see anything, let alone racing horses at a distance. By the time focus was achieved, the horses were long gone. My left eye is longer sighted than my right. Telescopes are unworkable for me. No one believes this fact. Correcting me to manage such objects is a complete waste of my time. So I pretend, to shut others up about the problem that seems to be connected in an unfathomable way with my dyslexic tendencies not to see things in front of me. Microscopes are usable. Stained slides and light make identification easy.

Both Molly and I suffered from photophobia, where strong or too much glare can trigger migraines. Are all these symptoms related or separate? Molly was not in any way dyslexic but she did not have the proper balance to ride a bike. A symptom of my dyspraxia. No freedom for girls.

Two bouts with viral pneumonia left Angus at death's door. Fred gave the doctor permission to try a new drug on Angus. Success. Angus was skeletal.

'The doctor thinks your brother would benefit from living in the country. The decision is Angus's. If he wants to live in the country, we will.' The country? Help! Life was hard enough for me in Ascot Vale where no one noticed me. Not the country. How could I survive in a country town? Thank goodness they did not want to farm. My body could not cope. A country school. No thank you. How would I fit in? Thankfully, Angus did not want to shift.

No doubt about it. However, Angus then started to eat comfort food and he became a tad overweight. Negative emotions hidden by comfort food. Molly never worried over-much about our weight. She was narked with her maternal grandfather, the third son of our mad Protestant Irish male ancestor, for passing on to her his large boned physique and his arthritis. Molly was a good cook. Slices of homemade cake to be consumed after school. Dessert after every evening meal. 'Eat everything on your plate, or no dessert.' Comfort food. Angus was being called fat at school. So humiliating! The great benefit from being undiagnosed with dyslexia and dyspraxia is that no one called me dumb, lazy or clumsy. Angus blamed Molly. Molly was puzzled. Angus was not eating any more food than usual. She did not feed him as much. Yet he was still putting on weight. Fred gave Angus an allowance. He spent most of his allowance on buying huge blocks of Kraft Cheddar Cheese. Nothing stopped Angus's affair with Kraft cheese. He seemed to grow out of the problem. Molly was unaware of the allowance or the Kraft cheese addiction. One of Molly's rules was 'Never tell tales.' Tales became secrets in my head. Averted verbal storms.

Gambling

Growing up, the lure of a monkey bar or high slide was always a gamble for me. Molly's family all gambled.

All her siblings seemed to be engaged in a never-ending game of gender warfare, undeclared but relentless. The sisters exchanged secrets. The men, for the most past, completely unaware. Although Boy had issues at times with his wife. All families face conflict whether from without or within. Molly was a frustrated veterinarian. Denied university because of being a girl, forced to attend an accounting course her elder sister rejected. Molly worked in the Accounts section and Fred in the Town Clerks office of Melbourne City Council. Fred followed his passion for soldiering, leaving Molly to cope with a broken leg and ill mother-in-law.

Hardly a fair division of labour.

Angus was beating me in a physical fight. I threw a pair of scissors at him that stuck in the window ledge. Molly slapped my face. 'That a child of mine should be jealous!' She had to talk me out of my well laid plan to leave home. Would my experiences have been any better if I had been born a generation later? Well, not necessarily. My listening skills were improved by listening to the radio. Reading aloud and reciting poetry and tongue twisters all helped me cope with schooling. Would I have been diagnosed? Probably not. Dyslexic/dyspraxic children still remain undiagnosed. Molly would have been swamped with shame and humiliation if I had been diagnosed. Her disdain was apparent to me, resulting in me choosing not to rock the boat to keep me out of trouble. My reality never matched their expectations. Keeping my own counsel, my salvation.

Odds and Sods

Flipping through magazines gives me most of the information I need about which item to read. A speed reading course helped me, but slow reading never bothered me, unlike my constant failure at remembering names. If a book is really boring, reading comes easier by reading the last chapter first. Reading words backwards is often easy. Searching pages of letters to discover words is easy. Maze puzzles are enjoyable. Otherwise, games hold no interest for me.

The Letter 'D' Has Been Important in My Life

Discipline to cope with dyslexia and dyspraxia.
Determination to defeat dyspraxia's results in my body.
Delusional thinking is banished by accepting
and finding ways around my limitations.
Delight at my success. Access to other realities.
Dissipation of any depressive tendencies.
Discovering many aspects of myself
while writing this book.

CLAIRE MOORE

Disabilities accepted and overcome.
Discoveries unending living with my Butterfly Mind.
Dyslexia develops other skills.
Dyspraxia leaves drastic results.
Disadvantages become challenges.
Delusion thinking reveals.
Despair vanishes.
Delight at accomplishments.

Claire Moore 2/10/2020

University

Daughters don't go to university. They attend secretarial college to become legal secretaries. Doomed to clerical positions.

Disillusioned housewife. While at a South Melbourne Neighbourhood House Professor Max Charlesworth encouraged mature age students to enrol in Deakin University Off-Campus studies. My application was accepted. One subject a year for nine years. Reading for each essay. One essay at a time. Dyslexia meant my essays were proofread. Erratic spelling. Essay copies had different spelling mistakes. Essay writing a formula similar to a recipe.

> Introduction, paragraphs for and against the topic, and conclusion.
> More than one copy of an essay meant different mistakes in each copy.
> The joy of erratic spelling.
> Proofreading was essential. Fred proofread all my essays. In an essay in Religious Studies, in

CLAIRE MOORE

the first draft 'belief' was misspelt right through
the essay, placing the 'e' before the 'i'.
Learning to ask questions about the
chosen essay topic a must.
Attending all tutorials vital.
University study was a very rewarding challenge.
Unlike most schools, universities sometimes
do help dyslexic students.
It is important to ask for extensions if needed.
Enjoy the challenge.
A subject at a time was all I could
manage. Otherwise chaos.
It took me nine years to complete my degree.
A double major in Australian History,
Theologies and Religion.
Everyone said I could not.

BUT I DID

Claire Moore 10/2/2022

Dyslexia and Learning

Travelling to Prahran and back via two trains to work in an estate agency as a junior clerk took time. Sitting in the old red rattler carriages. On hot days, with both doors open. When in motion the heat decreased. The trains smelt stale. Many people did not use deodorants. Sitting opposite men who hid behind their *Herald* evening newspapers. Staring at the headlines that faced me, sometimes I would not be able to make sense of them. My focus was then to keep looking until it made sense to me. It never occurred to me that this was a dyslexic symptom of mine. I remember imagining that dyslexic people do this, but thought nothing more. Molly claimed, 'Reading someone else's paper from the back is very rude.' So lucky that the headlines eventually made sense to me. Other dyslexics are not so fortunate, reinforcing the fact that symptoms of dyslexia and dyspraxia vary so much from individual to individual.

A dyslexic sailor who used Morse code demonstrated that discipline, determination and the correct help would cure his problem, as recorded in *Radio Girl* by David Dufty.

To someone like me, I failed to draw streetscapes, having no conception of distances. A Grade Six art teacher informed me I could not draw because of my problems with space.

A friend's son cannot spell. In his case, success is getting the first and last letter of a word right. However, he only needs to be given an oral instruction or see something done to be able to replicate these instructions. Welding and building are his forte. His mother fought his teachers at school who insisted that he was not dyslexic. Another education failure due to incorrect teaching. He is very competent with digital things. All of us learn differently.

Promotion

Gaining a promotion, working for the Melbourne City Council, Fred received a house in Newmarket as part of his salary. Molly suggested that we extend the garage in Ascot Vale to accommodate a council car. Molly enjoyed her home in Ascot Vale.

Fred gave Angus the choice of secondary schools, private and public. Angus chose University High School because of the school's high academic reputation. Unfortunately, the school residential pool for students did not include Ascot Vale. Newmarket and Kensington met residential qualifications for the school. The Ascot Vale property was sold.

Packing up the house was a huge job, with Molly in charge. Standing in the kitchen doorway overlooking a back porch, I watched as Molly climbed a wooden ladder to wash already clean wooden boards. Why? I watched in horror as the ladder did the splits. Molly broke a leg. Weeks in a wheelchair, unable to walk until seen by an old fashioned osteopath, Molly was under an immense amount of stress. While organising moving our dog had died. Unfortunately, years later, we discovered that Molly only thrived in Ascot Vale where she would easily interact with friends and family. Fred had been born in Kensington. We were welcomed by the Parkers who ran a grocery store. Gordon Cairncross and his family welcomed Angus into their family. Gordon was Fred's deputy. Molly was in charge of unpacking. Hated delegating.

Angus enjoyed both the cattle markets and University High School.

Fred, an able administrator, earned every cent the council paid him.

Parental Patterns

Neither Fred nor Molly shared my butterfly mind. Nor did any of my relations that knew me. Leaving me the only butterfly mind in the family. Molly insisted on me being truthful all the time while simultaneously failing to be honest with me. Fred never commented. He tended to tell me the truth. Some of Molly's thought patterns.

Molly never imagined a problem would not be solved. She taught me that the only problems to worry about were problems that could not be fixed, although time had a way of managing all problems. A feminist in philosophy was Molly. I discovered a copy of *The Second Sex* by Simone de Beauvoir. Molly held respect for others. No denigrating Indigenous people. No avoiding talking to Catholics because they were Catholics. This was the 1950s and '60s where Protestants and Roman Catholics often did not talk to each other. Molly demanded, and gave, respect. Close to her father, she could plan and build, paint.

Nothing was beyond her abilities. Pruning, garden planning gave her immense joy. Everyone loved Molly. Politicians and councils were bombarded with her letters about her concerns.

Fred, a cynic, thought all the letter writing a waste of time. He never tolerated fools. Especially in his children. He came from a position of integrity with a strong belief in law and order. Believed in due process. An ex-soldier, army mad as a boy and young man. Molly was in charge of discipline. Fred worked.

'Don't upset your father when he arrives home tired.' Fred was ignorant of a lot of our family life but he did not desire to be bothered with us.

Molly was big on threats. Her verbal abuse was constant, forming audio tapes in my head that need to be silenced.

'You'll never amount to anything.' What a challenge.

When out.

'Misbehave and I'll wipe the floor with you.' How could she, I wondered.

'Stand up straight or I'll have you confined in a brace.' A strange way to heal undiagnosed scoliosis and lordosis.

'Never lie to me. Your punishment will be worse if you lie.' Yet she lied to me.

'You give your enemies the advantage by showing your thoughts and emotions in your eyes. That must stop!' I wondered how.

'An untidy slut.' Labelled with an ugly word.

'From gutter to gutter in three generations.' Who, besides me, was in the gutter? Great-Aunt Susie was buried in a paupers' grave in Fawkner Cemetery, near Nan and Pop's grave. Was that the gutter? Her family disowned her. Who else? Do I really want anybody to love me like my mother? In my book *Poems from a Butterfly Mind*, below is the last verse of 'Words that Haunt'.

> Dysfunctional words.
> More dangerous than dyslexia.
> Dyspraxia attacks my body,
> Nervous system — mind.
> Dysfunctional words attack my soul.
>
> *Claire Moore 22/11/2020*

Nan abused her daughters on all levels. A granddaughter who lived with Nan endured being hit with the back of a hairbrush. Blackmailed by Nan into silence until my aunt, the girl's mother, turned 90.

'Well, it was so long ago, dear.' A five-minute wonder. No one listened. Molly and Nan, both long dead, but family patterns were emerging. Molly thought she could cure my sensitivities and toughen me up with verbal abuse. To withstand Molly's criticisms, Angus and I had to be tough. Fighting my parents for equal rights within the family helped obscure my dyslexia and dyspraxia. Again there were no words to describe my continual falls, dropping objects, other than 'clumsy klutz' or 'clumsy Claire'. No one ever wondered why my co-ordination and balance were such a problem for me. Molly felt she had enough problems without more from me. All my fault. Get on with it.

The house seemed to run like a military camp. Meals at certain times on the dot. Easy to remember rules. Verbal abuse if you forgot, Molly theoretically believed in the rights of women. Dysfunctional family patterns impossible to escape. Unending verbal abuse to toughen me up! No crying allowed. Girls paid a price for being born the wrong sex. Meals a daily ritual as was the housework.

Reading books, being thought of as literate, disguised and obliterated any investigation into learning difficulties. Not just being able to read but to discuss books. Political and social material gleaned from radio and newspapers meant I could participate in social and political discussion around the dinner table. Burying my head in a book meant that I would be left in peace to read. Historical novels, fiction of all sorts, non-fiction books. Being a bookworm, one of my few talents. Books taught me a lot. They still do. Without being taught phonics, how could I read. Phonics are a far from ideal way to spell. Better erratic spelling than appalling spelling for me. So blessed to be able to read. Some dyslexics may never read. They must be encouraged to use their other skills and intelligence. Not allowed to disappear. Many who are illiterate end up in prison. Money spent on identifying and aiding all dyslexics with personal aids, etc., in education would lead to less money needed in the prison system.

Ritual Meals at Newmarket

As the Superintendent of Abattoirs and Cattle Markets, Fred administered both on behalf of the Melbourne City Council and was a very busy man. He came home for lunch when working, thus eating up even more of Molly's free time. Information arrived at the dinner table we could all have done without. 'Remember George, the Judas sheep?' How could I forget. The one taught to eat lamb chops. How could we forget?

'Well, today he was accidentally slaughtered. No one remembered to inform the new slaughterman that he was not to kill George. The men are very upset.'

'Claire, can you spell transubstantiation?'

'TRANS SUB STANT IAT ION.'

'Well done, daught.'

Aced by me 98 per cent of the time, Fred threw long syllable words at me to catch so I could succeed. Neither of us knew it was the little words that trip me up. Although I can misspell long words too. Molly occasionally mouthing the letters at me was unnecessary. Fred was still throwing words at me to spell the week he died. He really believed he was improving my spelling ability, ignoring the fact that words I may spell one day but not the next.

'Did one of the drovers really call his dog across Epsom Road in front of a car?

'Yes. It was an old dog. He told the driver he owed him the price of a working dog. It is an old trick. These things happen. Life is tough, particularly for working dogs.' Greed unlimited.

Molly caught Susie eating her flowers again. She slipped off her tether, never making a sound, and into Molly's prize blooms.

'Smart Susie. The only lamb we've been able to raise.'

Sheep drop their lambs in the yards and are driven on elsewhere. Molly sent Pedro, our council gardener, to save those he could. A lot died from scours — diarrhoea in animals.

Pedro grew up on a Ukrainian farm.

'Black tea, missus. Black tea.' The tannin stops the scours. It worked! She really loved Molly's flowers.

'Poor Susie thinks she is human.' Never interested in the sheep running past the fence line to the abattoirs.

'Thank God for that!'

'She was shorn with Teddy this morning at my deputy's place.' Teddy was a grown sheep belonging to Fred's deputy. They lived across Epsom Road from us. Teddy, their pet lamb, fell in love at first sight. Susie looked down her nose at him, completely ignoring his existence. It was funny seeing her reaction.

'No Moreton Bay figs tonight.' Releasing her from her tether, I lied. 'Figs, Susie.' Off she ran like a greyhound. Me in pursuit. She took one look in her manger and turned to race out. I was too quick for her and shut her in for the night. Turning the third garage into her stable was a good idea. I loved running my hands through her fleece, the lanolin felt good. She was supposed to be a Merino-Leicester throwback cross, whatever that is. Susie and the rescued feral cats made life in the cattle markets somewhat bearable.

Pedro was banished from the mansion garden because he replanted Molly's annuals three times. Molly preferred the small plants in the front, gradually ending with the tall plants at the rear. Pedro preferred the reverse order. After three seasons of this, Molly put her foot down. Pedro was promoted to install and maintain a vegetable garden in the abattoir grounds where poor Susie was buried after swallowing a sliver of wood. Pedro spoke good English, except when he disagreed with Molly, then his English seemed to vanish.

The trauma of life at the abattoirs and cattle markets seemed unending. A stressful environment that increased my undiagnosed dyslexic tendencies. The stress was increased by living in an inconvenient council mansion. Two back doors. One led to an outside bathroom of huge proportions. Painted a bright yellow. Molly hated yellows used as house paint. The toilet resided next door. No connecting door. Eaves were some shelter on rainy days. From the front door, down the main hallway, two doors on the left and four on the right. The master bedroom, plus a magnificent lounge-dining room of Victorian vintage occupied the left of the house. A small hall ended in a walk-in pantry with the door on the left opening to a tiny kitchen, where a huge window overlooked the tennis court. Stove and oven in the far wall. A small, two-seater table that could be folded up sat between the hall and scullery doors. On the other side, near the window, lurked another walk-in pantry. In the scullery, a huge gas hot water service tank sulked in front of a long bench with one sink staring at a painted brick wall. Light flooded in from a long window, opposite the sink. A second back door led out into an asphalt courtyard. Dull brown linoleum covered the kitchen areas. Opposite the main bedroom was a huge rumpus room with dormer windows painted a revolting lime green, teamed with lime green linoleum. No taste. Decorating by council on the cheap, I would imagine. I inherited the brown room. Brown felted floor covering, huge dark brown holland blind. My parents donated their double wardrobe that hid behind a brown door.

Twice a week, on market days. Early morning. *Crack! Crack!* – the crack of stock whips woke me. Men swearing, working dogs barking, cattle bellowing along the street as they were ushered into the cattle markets through a gate bordering our fence. On sheep days, the sheep at times seemed too scared to bleat. Their little hooves hitting the asphalt like machine gun bullets fired in quick succession. On damp market days, the stench of stale urine, soiled straw, lay in the air. On the days of hot northerly winds, dry straw and manure wafted along on the wind. Sheep dogs jumping on yarded sheep backs. Susie would have hated such an indignity. To get the cattle off the street, the mansion was demolished. Added to Molly's stress was the task of organising, by phone, the subbies for the deaf builder for our new home behind the abattoirs. The council exploited her good will and gardening abilities. The huge eyes of beef cattle, staring over our back fence, awaiting slaughter on Monday, haunt me still.

'They don't know.' The stench of death was not a mystery to them. Of course they knew. Stress of animal suffering was a constant part of my life. Now, I cannot eat red meat.

Growing Up

Writing this book has been confronting on many levels. Dealing with my conflicted relationship with my parents, a struggle for fairness ensued, dwarfing my spelling trials. Falling over was just normal for me. Shameful and humiliating. None of my cousins were clumsy.

At primary school, children of my own age scared me, particularly boys. Molly forbade me talking to stable boys. A cousin included me in a walk with two stable boys. All very innocent, I did not speak a word. A most peculiar girl. Not obeying an order, if caught, resulted in a cloak of disapproval enfolding me. All it took was a look. You had overstepped a line and must pay the consequences. Verbal retribution was terrifying. A weapon that demolished self. Even my brother would say, 'Don't be so stupid,' in front of others if I held a different viewpoint. An effective way to silence me. My immediate family were great conversationalists on social matters, world affairs, history, geography and politics. General knowledge was important. Feelings were never mentioned.

Fred ignored his daughter who possessed no talents he could boast about at the office. Molly's disapproval was apparent, both verbal and non-verbal. Fred never bothered to talk to me about anything personal at all. Personal messages were passed on by Molly.

'Claire, your father is very pleased with you.' Truly? Every eighteen months to two years he would deign to pat me on the head. 'You'll pass, with a push.' Alternatively, 'You'll pass, in a crowd.' High praise indeed from my father. My reaction to such words was to ignore them. Encouraged to read non-fiction and fiction books as approved by Molly. Both my parents loved and promoted the reading of Shakespeare's plays. Comics were deemed by Molly as too corrupting for us to read. Molly's youngest sister, Jean, bought comics for her children. While Molly and Jean talked, I caught up on Superman, the Phantom, the Lone Ranger, Batman and Bugs Bunny, Mickey Mouse, Donald Duck and others. Reading comics had the advantage of keeping me out of my cousins' way.

Writing was a continuing battle during primary school. Molly kept a badly printed card from my first primary school days. The letters were wobbly and correct but up and down. A straight line impossible. Letter writing, for me, was a problem. As a child, when presented with a pen plus paper and told to write a thank you note, my mind would go blank. The mechanics I knew, address, date, content then 'Love from Claire'. An immense amount of struggle went into the content of these small letters. Trying hard not to make mistakes meant rewriting correctly. My aunt Doreen and uncle George were the main recipients of my woeful letters. Doreen never wrote letters. As she read manuscripts for a publishing company, I assumed she could write well. Concentration was needed for learning grammar and punctuation marks. Full stops were easy. Commas less so. Where did they go? Reading revealed books full of grammar and spelling. Grammar slipped into my mind at times. Stories conjured visions in my brain. English mastery took much longer for me. Grammar relentless. Spelling pesky. Indexes and bibliographies were a waste of space. Dictionaries to be avoided. They required correct spelling. In secondary school, spelling mistakes always lowered my marks in other subjects. Knowing many subjects well, this seemed unfair. Molly's expertise in speech problems sorted out any mispronunciations of mine. In short order. Luckily tongue twisters were easy and enjoyable for me. She made me read aloud. Pronunciations differ at times from person to person! Listening to surrounding company always gives a clue. Speech and singing lessons at Penleigh helped. Stuttering can still occur if my brain cannot pronounce a word. Spelling was never my focus. Such a focus would have increased my stress levels, creating shame and humiliation at my continual failures. During my teens, my letter writing improved. As my composition improved, my handwriting began to deteriorate. Biro pens did not help. At times, my writing can be illegible, even to me. Letters flowed to Doreen in Sydney, Molly's relatives in New Zealand and friends overseas. Spelling in these letters was never an issue with me. No one I ever wrote to commented, possibly because they had to decipher my scrawl.

Dyslexia is complex. Different symptoms common. Dyspraxia does not always occur with dyslexia. Combinations are endless, appearing to be unique to each individual. Stress is a prerequisite for me to write dangling sentences. Dangling sentences now invade my speech more than my writing. Most people fail to notice. This usually happens at the end of a sentence. If at the beginning of a sentence, no one would know what I am talking about. Mental chaos at times, but never for long as different realities and points of view emerge from chaos.

Shattered Elbow

Tripping over a rough patch on a South Melbourne unmade footpath, I landed on my left elbow. The elbow shattered. Overwhelming pain. I went to Prince Henry's Hospital. Waited four days to have the elbow reset. This slowed healing. Pins removed privately, 18 months later at a local hospital, before being referred to a plastic surgeon, who referred me on to another orthopaedic surgeon, for another elbow operation to prevent my left arm from lying across my stomach. Mr Simon Bell restored function to my elbow. I am very grateful for his aid.

Returning from a day at the Werribee Races, falling over, landing on my right side. I sustained concussion and a fractured right elbow. The local emergency doctor put my arm in a sling, telling me to exercise. Upon a request for a referral to Mr Bell, he informed me that the specialist would not see me. Upon arrival home, Mr Bell's receptionist informed that if we came straight down to his rooms in Brighton, he would see me. Half an hour later, all exercise for my right elbow was cancelled until further notice. The fracture healed without any trouble.

Concussions were common. My penchant for falling over has never made me fear falling. Falling over has been such a part of my life. In earlier life, the falls Molly knew about were attributed to my weak ankles. Running often resulted in falls, twisted ankles, skinned knees and hands. Catching balls, thrown without warning, was impossible. Skipping was manageable, but not French and German (two skipping ropes being held at each end by girls who kept the two ropes in rotation to be jumped over). Occasional success. Hoppy — playing hopscotch — meant balancing on one foot. Always a challenge but mostly manageable.

An accumulation of failures made me realise that the terms 'normal' or 'excellent' did not apply to me. Trying hard meant catastrophes. Feelings of being a half person intensified. Escaping punishment for my imperfections helped me to exploit and rely on my perceptions, along with my problem-solving abilities. Being with Molly could result in furore. After a piano lesson, Nan asked me to pick up her tripe from the butcher in Charles Street. Mission completed. Nan gave me a shilling as a reward. Stupidly, I told Molly. The trudge back to Nan's to return the shilling after 6 pm.

'You should do Nan's messages for nothing.' A pleasant surprise from Nan resulted in Molly confirming the awareness that my work was of no value to anyone.

No bioreceptors in my head means at times my head comes into contact with hard objects. Car doors, bedheads, cupboard doors, shelves. Concussions from accidents. Whiplash, not my fault. Fractures, a hole in my head, all mount up, creating a distrust of my body. Walking still tends to be looking for cracks or things that can trip me up. Trust in my body is always a work in progress. Muscle stiffness limits neck mobility. My neck problems mean I can only type for two hours at a time. Piano practice lasts between 30 minutes and an hour at a time before my neck muscles complain. Salvation has always been manipulative therapies. Osteopathy, cranial osteopathy, chiropractic, remedial massage with a qualified therapist. Exercise has always been vital for mobility. Swimming a mile two or three times a week helped until undone by a chlorine allergy. Walking alone, or with my dogs, strengthens my body. Painkillers are not a viable option. At times acupuncture has aided with any pain problems. Self-hypnosis, plus meditation, can also aid with pain in many individuals.

Living with Dyspraxia

Dyspraxia causes me untold problems with my body. Traumas induced by falls, concussion and broken bones become buried in my body. Pain is often a companion. My parents continued to blame weak wrists, weak ankles, small feet and small hands. Worst of all, Molly repeatedly labelled me 'careless Claire'. All my fault. No extenuating circumstances. Carelessness being responsible for my falls. My co-ordination and balance required constant attention from me. Six years of body building at Michael Hunt's Men's Gymnasium, swimming laps afterwards at the City Baths lessened back pain and muscle strain. Trauma never leaves my body. My experiences of all trauma changes. No longer does challenging my body seem a good idea. Clumsiness and carelessness defined me as a sporting failure as a child. Learning to trust my body is an unending challenge. Avoiding areas of competition gave relief from anxiety.

Dyspraxia means 35 to 45 minutes of morning exercises to stretch all muscles, fascia, tendons and ligaments using Pilates exercises followed by 10 to 20 minutes of Dragon Gate Chi Gong exercises each morning and night. Chi Gong exercises strengthen body organs and their functions. All my exercises have been prescribed by practitioners, to improve my balance, co-ordination and health daily, resulting in less pain from my spine, hips and neck problems. Twenty years of Pilates lessons, ten years of Chi Gong, having no concept of my body in space means often being told to straighten my body by practitioners. Chiropractic treatments, bi-weekly remedial massage by a qualified therapist, all keep my body mobile, strengthening my core muscles and limiting falls. Walking also aids my mobility.

Molly and Fred both gave me the discipline and determination that aids me in managing my dyspraxia. Other invaluable aids have been acupuncture and kinesiology. Both have decreased pain levels and increased my body's resistance to shocks. Working on emotional insecurities caused by dyslexia and dyspraxia, I have learnt not to compare myself to others who seem perfect. An occasional slip occurs sometimes. They seem fit, strong and athletic. Success to me, on an emotional level, now is not a problem. There is no desire for me to replicate the achievements of others. Competition still holds no appeal. Co-operation does.

Dyslexia and dyspraxia have taught me to take what is needed from everything I encounter, to improve my mind and body. Writing these stories has been confronting on all levels. Working through the problems has helped heal issues with Fred and Molly. Accepting that I 'am as I am' releases stresses and anxiety. My butterfly mind flits here and there, seeking for aids to my body and ways to solve problems. Problems may be long term but eventually are overcome. A tensile strength of mind aids in my determination and discipline. Even as a child, resilience has always been within me.

'Get up and get on with it. Cry and you cry alone.' Lessons learnt early that strengthened me.

Many of my challenges were my secrets. Molly never knew. An unstoppable force sometimes. Her determination for me to include a ruler made of different native New Zealand timbers in one of my geography projects would lead me to losing marks, being overkill, a present from her trip to New Zealand when her last aunt died. Molly's happiness came before my marks! Arguing was too undignified. She never argued with anyone. Verbal battles in her parental home, and Fred's, were common. Being her daughter meant doing as Molly decreed. Keeping my head down and my mouth shut most of the time seemed to work. Fred possessed a biting tongue. Preferences for boys were always a sore point with me. Unconditional love was lavished on me by Sonia whom I called

So-So, and Mandrake, my black Labrador. Neither ever criticised me. They gave unending approval and support. The dogs provided me with security. They were my loyal confidants and companions, who could be trusted with all my secrets. They never rejected or belittled me. They did not prefer boys. Their greatest gift, unconditional love.

Angus at university meant me sharing a car with him. What fun! In the morning I'd pick him up and he would drive me to work in the city. In the evening waiting times varied. Rarely on time. After waiting an hour, I caught public transport to his flat in Carlton.

'He's just left to pick you up. You should have waited.' Waiting for two hours on a street corner? I don't think so. Gender bias again seemed more important to me than my erratic spelling and constant falls. There seemed to be no commonality between the two. Losing balance, poor co-ordination, twisting ankles, all separate occurrences. Both parents seemed preoccupied with my spelling abilities. Not me. Most of my clerical positions were in accounts sections. Reception desks at Jessie McPherson Private Hospital and Royal Prince Alfred Hospital in Sydney. Typing was limited. Health claim forms and bills were handwritten at the time. Although being retrenched from Melbourne City Libraries Administration was a direct result of me no longer being able to pack and transport boxes of books when administration changed offices.

Not only could I fall down stairs, I can fall up stairs. My body was an unsafe place to be. A disability that fails to inspire self-confidence. Remember, this is about my dyspraxia, no one else's. Sports such as mountain climbing could cause falls. Parachuting could wreck my spine. Water skiing was impossible. Nordic skiing saved the day. Pomas (single person ski transport) and T-bars a nightmare. Yachting, clambering around decks, was too painful. Tennis became impossible. The force of a ball hitting my racquet created pain in spine and arms. I was running for a train on platform 12 at Flinders Street station on the way home from work, in a very smart pair of high heels, which resulted in me falling flat on my face, learning the hard way that high heels were not for me. A desire to be a florist was thwarted by weak fingers and wrists. Childproof articles led to huge frustrations. An enormous amount of frustration was pushed down into my body and subconscious, released by counselling and body work. Fingers on my right hand at times failing, so whatever is in them falls to the ground. Sometimes I imagine this is my right hand's protest at being made to write. Accidents were frequent when I was hurrying not estimating the time needed without having to run for trains and trams. My butterfly mind races at great speed. My dyspraxic body does not. When cooking, there is always too much food. Estimating how many veggies or fruit ends up perishing. Not being able to estimate correctly, erring on the side of too much being better than not enough. Not expecting falls to occur means the falls shock my system. Time sitting or lying is still needed before attempting to get back on my feet. My main aim is to reduce pain and restore function to my body before diagnosis. Ten years of Hatha Yoga, never getting past exercise ten. No other Yoga school would touch me because of my bad spine, falsely imagining they may be sued. Trauma from falls remains buried in my body's memory. For me, writing has aided me in overcoming many challenges.

Dyspraxia and the Bank

Aged 18, I began working at the Australia and New Zealand bank in Bay Street, Port Melbourne. On my first day, the senior clerk took me outside and turned me to face the beach.

'You need to go down Bay Street to the National Bank to pick up the scales, then bring them back here, to balance the books.' My heart sank.

'You don't need scales to balance the books.' Not being a fool, the staff left me alone after that.

Friday morning's paperwork for a money transfer had to be taken into the head office to enable money to be transferred to a parent company in England. A green tramways bus, belching diesel fumes, carried me into Flinders Street. Walking up to Collins Street, opposite the then new modern AMP building. A Victorian banking chamber of elegance graced the ANZ building, with a mezzanine floor, white marble floor, banisters and stairs formed a graceful frame to two functional lifts. A male operator controlled each lift. The stairs were good exercise. The paperwork safely delivered, an easy task. Walking back to the lifts. One was on the top floor, the other not near. Down the marble stairway I walked. Sunshine lighted the stairs from a long casement window. Feeling happy, I walked down to the ground floor. On the third last step, my feet slipped from under me, landing me flat on my bottom, my legs stretched out in front of me. Pain instantly assaulted my spine. The accident was witnessed by the kind lift-man on the right side of the stairs. An irate manager arrived.

'Why did you not take the lift?'

'The other lift-man refuses to transport young people to and from the mezzanine floor. He claims they need to use their legs. The right lift had not been available.' His rant stopped as did his attempt to blame me for my fall. The bank agreed to pay for my medical treatment. In X-rays my spine looked like a mouse had eaten pieces out of all my vertebrae.

'Mrs Herd, your daughter is lucky not to have been paralysed from bone particles dislodged from her spine. Your daughter has Scheuermann's disease of the spine.' Possibly activated by the fall, don't know what the cause is, thought to be inherited. Her GP thought as much.

'She'll have to wear a neck to coccyx brace. No lifting of heavy objects. Two weeks off, then we will see.' My world shrank to the house. Spinal manipulations three times a week with my GP.

'You do well, Claire. Never make a sound.' Sitting sideways across a hard-backed chair, my hands clasped behind my neck, holding an elbow in each hand, he put a knee up to my neck and cracked my spine all the way down to my coccyx. What was there to say. He has my gratitude forever for preventing me developing a Scheuermann's disease hump on my spine, thanks to his manipulations.

Returning to work, my back injury was not obvious.

'Would you take the ledger tray down to the ledger machine?'

'Do it yourself,' said the teller, causing me to burst into tears and my nose to bleed uncontrollably. The accountant then explained my predicament to the teller. My orthopaedic surgeon was furious with the bank's attitude.

'Refer them to me.' The bank staff could not, or refused to, comprehend my back pain. Thankfully, my resignation was with the manager.

My specialist refused to send me to a physiotherapist. He did not believe in them, he referred me to Michael

Hunt's Men's Gymnasium, for men, at the City Baths. They accepted me as a client. Fred paid my fees.

In later life, not informing Pilates teachers of my dyslexia led to misunderstandings. However, you can inform others of your dyslexia. But lack of knowledge of the problem, others assume reading to be the only problem. Then mention dyspraxia. Many individuals had no concept of the problem at all.

Questions That May Help after a Fall

Did you just drop down? Did you trip and drop?

Sit still, let the shock settle. Notice how and why.

Were your shoes adequate for support? What action tipped your balance? Did anything get in the way? Did you twist an ankle? Did you land on your hands? How does your head feel? No noticeable soreness?

You can get up. Continue your day.

Soreness arrives, have a shower. Keep warm, put legs up. Topical rubs to lessen pain. Try small movements. If no pain, continue. Bad pain, go to a doctor or emergency department, particularly if concussed. Take charge. Never again take that fall.

Why continual exercise?

My body would not be flexible. Not to exercise, for me, is not to exist. If you don't really enjoy exercise, try to find one that suits your mind and body.

Researching my memories of a dysfunctional childhood has enabled me to confront unresolved issues in a positive way. Researching my history of dyspraxia and dyslexia seems to have unleashed my erratic spelling. While two falls have occurred, with occasional mental confusion, continual falling creates confusion, adds to the chaos.

Understanding how and why.

Family may encourage, or be able to liberate the problem, or no help at all!

Dyspraxia Theory

Dyspraxia is thought to be caused by problems with the motor function of the brain. The planning function fails to follow through with action. Symptoms range from mild to severe. Symptoms may be varied or solitary. Problems seem to be caused by the brain's inability to plan in correct sequence, whereas most brains seem to automatically manage to plan seamlessly.

A general lack of co-ordination makes balance difficult, excluding me from bike riding, golf, leading to nightmares in many sporting situations. Ballet becomes impossible.

No co-ordination or faulty co-ordination can lead to continual falls. Demands to try harder lead to a feeling of frustration because I am trying hard.

Sometimes dyslexia and dyspraxia combine. This is true for me. Many individuals may only be challenged by dyslexia or dyspraxia.

Helping Teenagers and Adults With Dyslexia

Luckily for me, I can read. In lectures, taking notes aided me in understanding the topic.

That is how I work, *but all of us are different.*

Writing essays means studying the question to decipher the correct answer. This may take time. With multiple choice essays, my approach is to choose the topic that is most familiar, then read for the essay you have chosen to answer. Underline your textbooks with pencil. Take notes on large ruled cards. Write down source and page of each card. Read for your essay topic.

A first step is to brainstorm all the information needed on a huge piece of paper. Then arrange topics into similar groups. A separate card for each group. Group together arguments for and against the topic.

Draw mind maps of all paragraphs. Write each paragraph on a different lined card, then play with their positions in your essay.

Discover, and use, joining words that make your essay flow — conversely, it can be claimed, on the other hand.

Nevertheless, the list of words to choose is huge!

Conclusion may be written before the introduction. Write all quotes on cards with name of author, title, date and page number, published by whom, for your bibliography at the end of the essay. Then assemble the first draft of the essay. A science professor told me that to gain distinctions, write an essay seven times. By the end of six rewrites, you are well and truly fed up with the topic, but your final mark will improve, but such a strategy may not work for everyone.

Remember to gain permission from school or university authorities to have a good speller proofread for typos and spelling mistakes. My spelling mistakes seem never-ending.

Dyslexia limited my educational opportunities as a teenager. Not knowing why meant that at some level I thought of myself as a failure. Allow the luxury of wallowing for a day, then discover how to solve the problem from another perspective. Change always arrives in one form or another. Get on with your life.

Dyslexics who cannot master reading need the help of audio aids and personal aides in class. Oral questions need recording with answers. Exams need to be oral, with the help of a personal aide. Counselling is necessary to support dyslexics who are sane, not dumb or lazy.

The desire to learn is thwarted if you do not have the keys to learn. Confidence in one's own abilities vanishes. Help, let alone diagnosis, can be impossible to find.

Rudolph F Wagner, an American, notes Dr Erickson's comment that normal identity crises for adolescents are difficult. However, the dyslexic adolescent is always under stress. The US Navy believes that by using discipline, supervising all homework and always standing in front of the poor reading students, all the time, they can provide better instruction than public schools. They turn a second grade level reader into a reader capable of succeeding in Navy basic training over the basic five week course. [Wagner's book *Dyslexia and Your Child*, Chapter 10 'Dyslexia and the Adolescent' pp. 150–153.]

Diagnosed as dyslexic at 33, the knowledge enabled me to attend university successfully. The focus appears to be on reading and ability to write, other symptoms are overlooked. Feeling like a half person instead of being whole, accompanied me through 30 years of ignorance.

Don Tolman in his *Encyclopedia of Whole Food Medicine, Volume II*, suggests that the increasing incidents of dyslexia are an evolutionary change, developing new brain functions in many children.

'Dyslexia is a non-disease of today's formal academic and educational standards. Forte Numen is what I call dyslexia. It means "Strength of Genius" (p. 398).'

Many children who fail to crawl are warning parents of learning difficulties ahead. Almost a disposition for dyslexia. Why is this possibility ignored by parents, kindergarten teachers and the medical profession?

Undiagnosed Dyslexia in Others

Dyslexia today in Australia appears to be grossly underdiagnosed. There are many different ways people cope.

May, in her late 70s, was not diagnosed with dyslexia until after she turned 50. Her slow reading and poor arithmetic were, at times, punished by May being strapped before her class. She still experiences problems with distances.

The heroine in Penelope Janu's book, **Up On Horseshoe Hill,** *is a dyslexic farrier who has trouble reading and writing. Sometimes she can read, except when stressed. Her literacy skills fail. A friend does her books for her. She has trouble with shoelaces and tangles. As a character, she is a very well drawn picture of a dyslexic person. Diagnosed as a child, she could not master remedial tuition at times.*

Diagnosed as dyslexic at 40, a lady running a health food shop finds reading very difficult because her capital and normal letters all look the same. They tend to run together while punctuation is also difficult.

Recently, a neighbour lent me a copy of a memoir of her relationship with her first husband. Some names had capital letters, others did not. 'Oh, I can't be bothered with capitals,' she explained. Still a dyslexic symptom. Looking ahead at an object without seeing the object — another dyslexic symptom. The lady, in her mid-80s has never worried about her writing problems. Never diagnosed and never worried about capital letters. What a great attitude.

Expanding on a case of dyslexia previously mentioned.

In David Dufty's book **Radio Girl:**

An extraordinary story of Mrs MacKenzie, an electrical engineer, businesswoman and promoter of women's rights. Trainer of women, during World War II, who became signallers in Morse code accepted by the Australian Navy as professionals. The American army had their signalmen trained by her. Post war, a merchant sailor kept failing his exams to become a second officer. He kept failing the Morse code section of the course. Mrs Mac and her husband worked with this seaman, discovering that he suffered from Morse code dyslexia. She worked hard with the seaman until he passed the Morse code examination. Later he became a sea captain and merchant lawyer, Morse code dyslexia apparently his only symptom.

Many people with dyslexia are extremely intelligent people. A younger cousin was in the same class as a friend of mine.

'The teacher told me to help him with his arithmetic. He is so slow. I hit him with my ruler.' In his 70s, he still has poor writing and reading skills. He would never accept a dyslexic label. My cousin remains unaware that dyslexia exists. No wonder he had problems!

A remedial spelling class at the Council of Adult Education was revealing. Eight students, all of whom were dyslexic to some degree, all undiagnosed and shamed because they felt so dumb. By the end of the class, all experienced increased self-esteem. Many illiterate people are experts at disguising their problem. My spelling is still erratic.

A football trainer who could not write or read and no one knew. His strategies were excellent. Travelling to Heathrow airport, he could not read the signage about which train to take. Narrowing the choices to two lines, he guessed which train to take. Anxiety descended while he waited for the train to Heathrow. The stress was horrendous.

For an Italian man, illiterate in his own language, writing and reading in English was almost impossible. He tried too hard and became so frustrated with himself. Others in the class felt shame for being dumb. In reality, most experienced dyslexic symptoms.

Dyslexia takes many forms in differing situations. It is not easy to pigeonhole. Writing about reading failure seems very simplistic and fails to do justice to the complexity of dyslexic symptoms.

A friend's great-nephew is six. A middle child, he has been diagnosed with dyslexia. His mother and teacher are managing his condition. The mother has elected to refuse the miserly state aid. He is progressing well.

Dyslexic children can experience low boredom thresholds or drift off into daydreams. Teachers need more training in remedial work to be able to identify and aid children with dyslexia.

Teachers telling parents 'Not to worry, the child will grow into reading' can be a cop-out at times. In American schools, there seems to be more success at identifying dyslexic children and providing suitable aids. Individual carers are often part of the classroom scene. A long way from our classroom realities.

Boys are said to be more likely to have dyslexia than girls. In the past, I think that boys may have been easier to diagnose than girls. After all, girls were expected to marry, therefore education was not deemed essential. Or, perhaps, girls are much cleverer than boys at disguising the problem.

More Symptoms of Dyslexia

Eye movements see different shapes, sequences of letters, or numbers, which reverse or change, sometimes dance. Numbers and letters, at times, do not remain still. They disappear, grow, shrink and move. Punctuation marks and capital letters are missed because they become invisible or are ignored. Spelling is not helped when a computer program puts capital letters at the beginning of each line. Spelling varies from acceptable to erratic, perfection never obtainable. Whole words may be omitted or altered in both reading and writing.

Dyslexia, when in full flow, can encourage feelings of failure, inferiority, anger, frustration, that no matter how hard you try, you cannot succeed. Constant criticism from teachers, relatives, fellow pupils and parents intensifies feelings of failure and the unfairness of school and others' comments. You do not have the words to express your feelings. Success does not arrive. Fragile self-esteem is trampled, often by well-meaning individuals.

Dangling sentences escape unnoticed by my mind into existence. This occurs when the stress load becomes heavy. Speaking is reliant on sounds. Dyslexic ears often hear sound differently. False sounds can be heard. Sounds such as 'th' and 'ch' easy to mispronounce. Reading aloud is an impossible task. Sounds are softer, louder, nearer than the reality.

Dyslexia develops other skills. Gives access to other planes. Determination plus discipline overcomes the drastic results of dyspraxia. Delusional thinking revealed. Disadvantages become challenges. Discoveries unending. Delight at accomplishments.

Molly shared a dysfunctional relationship with me, but there were times of fun. Always a dog, sheep or cat for solace, love and companionship, providing unconditional love to a child whose actions were seen as an insult to her family. The animals' concern for me was not affected by me having dyslexia or dyspraxia. Total acceptance of me despite my perceived faults.

Respectability

The constant pressure to conform. Respectability was worshipped above compassion and reality. I had a friend, Mary, a slow reader, who struggled with arithmetic at school. Teachers, who knew she was struggling with reading and arithmetic, ignored her plight. Her first job was as a ledger machinist at a bank. The words were easy by then, she knew her figures. Later, working at a post office, written evaluations were required. She coped by studying how other officers wrote reports. Writing an essay for her is challenging. Mary's focus was on her strengths, not her weakness.

What symptoms belong to dyslexia, dyspraxia or both? Does this matter?

Left and Right Hand, Which Side Is Which?

Preschool, I could look to the right, look to the left and look to the right again and cross a road. Someone telling me to turn left or right was a totally different matter. A complete puzzle in fact. Watching other children and following their lead often saved the day. In desperation, Molly often wrote an L on my left hand. A great aid if I remembered to look. Walking down to primary school, the road was on my right side. Walking home, the road was then on my left side. Molly was concerned about this. Today I have to think which way to turn if ordered to turn left or right. My inability to turn left and right led me to being diagnosed as a dyslexic. When navigating in a car with friends, if I am navigating, they know when I say turn right or left to look at the way my hand and finger are pointing. My finger always points in the correct direction. Whoever I am navigating for knows this fact, although they have been known to forget with some amazing results. Difficulties in distinguishing between left and right is also a symptom of dyspraxia.

Reading a clock is always a challenge. Eyes that record the wrong time in my brain, usually an hour early. Has the meditation lasted for half an hour or five minutes?

Changing from imperial distances to metric measures is loathsome. I still think in imperial measures. Measuring distance can be problematic. Decimal currency was easy for me.

Eyes that sometimes miss objects. Ears that fail to hear some instructions. Fingers that go on strike. Prior receptors that fail to inform my head of danger. Touch is my weakest sense.

Not Listening

Today, at the Commonwealth Bank, while talking to a grandmother of a dyslexic boy, I realised that all my life I have been punished for not listening. As a dyslexic, the harder I focus on what you say, the more likely I am not to hear your instructions correctly.

Dyslexic children are often accused of not listening. At times, a vital word can be missed that generates failure in a classroom or at home. 'Now, young lady. Listen to me,' one of Molly's favourite sayings. A butterfly mind is easily distracted. Trying harder is not an option. Trying harder increased my inability to hear all your instructions clearly and correctly. My hearing can be erratic just like my spelling. Over 47 years, verbal abuse descended upon me for the misperceived sin of not listening.

On a list of crimes, not listening or misunderstanding are not mentioned. Yet children and adults with dyslexia or dyspraxia seem to be continually punished for such lapses. Luckily for me, Molly spoke clearly, as did Fred. Many teachers and parents fail to speak clearly, making life more difficult for their literate student, while their failure humiliates and shames the less literate in the class. Dyspraxia in Grade Five resulted in a huge ink blot after being told to write perfectly.

The message obviously reached my mind and intellect, while failing to reach my right hand. Trying very hard not to create an ink blot on my exercise book ensured that I did. The frustration at the anger at my failure became a bad memory buried somewhere in my body.

How to cope? My mind may read instructions or lessons differently to you. Or my mind may read as you do. Stress is a huge contributing factor in how my dyslexia manifests.

An accumulation of failures made me realise that the term 'normal' or 'excellent' did not apply to me. Trying hard meant catastrophes. Feelings of being a half person resurfaced and intensified. Escaping punishment for my lack of perfection helped me to rely on my perceptions and problem-solving abilities. Being honest often resulted in furore.

Dyslexia and dyspraxia are part of who I am. Without their presence, my development would have, perhaps, been easier. The toughness needed to survive a gift from both my parents.

The Joy of Computers

Two laptops are used by me for word processing. What could be easier, you may think. Well, no. Typing away on a laptop, saving half pages religiously, put the document to bed. In the morning, four pages have disappeared, filed by the computer elsewhere! How despicable! Found, saved elsewhere. Without aid, they would never have reappeared. My laptop crashed, the one that loved putting capital letters on the start of each line. Unasked for screens appear and if I press the wrong key, all disappear. Then the insert key completely fails to work and eats letters, willy-nilly. So, the delightful laptop crashes completely. Off to the computer shop to be fixed. A week without typing. Back it comes with a different programme that has to be relearnt. A new printer exclusively for my laptop helps. Then, another week, away the laptop goes and comes back with email access and the ability to hold a Zoom meeting (so the experts claim). The laptop would then need to be in the main computer room where the camera resides.

Oh, what fun! More challenges. Zoom meetings have silenced me, excluded me, occasionally included me, but have frustrated me immensely. One must have faith. Why?

'Computers save so much time.' Because of numerous neck and other injuries, standing at the computer has become an ergonomic way for me to type. The laptop resides on three large phone books. A Microsoft full length keyboard is attached to my laptop. Using a laptop keyboard leads to ergonomic disaster for my body. Using a mouse, for any computer, is not an option. My hand co-ordination creates all sorts of problems trying to set the arrow to click on the correct symbol. Attempting to align eyes with hand movements results in chance. Two hours computing time only. Five minutes of every half hour required. Difficult when absorbed in writing.

Spell check.

'Spell check surely fixes the problem,' a teacher commented.

'Well, no.' Spell check identifies some spelling mistakes. It does not correct words that are out of context. Examples — 'new' spelled as 'knew' or 'pray' spelled as 'prey'. The spell check on my IBM compatible uses American spelling. I prefer the English version where verandah is accepted, not corrected to veranda. This is without the mystery of what material is saved on what and where. Computers are, to me, an exercise in frustration.

Printer craziness. My new compact computer only uses black ink for word processing, refuses to obey instructions typed into the reauired format to print. Instructed to print one copy, the printer ran amok producing over 30 copies instead of one. After this incident, I became extraordinarily careful to ensure only one copy be printed. Yet again, the printer went into overdrive, producing excessive copies of one page again. Unstoppable by me, as if computer tantrums are not enough, now the printer loves to waste paper, print and my time. Incorrect misbehaving software may be the cause. A technical problem, not due to me. An added spur to my typing frustrations and delight with digital eauipment, confront all unresolved issues that need to be confronted in a positive way. Computer courses can add to confusion. They vary so much.

Researching my history of dyspraxia and dyslexia seems to have unleashed my erratic spelling, plus a dash of chaos.

Digital Delights

Digital things are very difficult for me. Most stories of intelligent dyslexic people are about **MALES** like Leonardo da Vinci.

A reject of the education system, David Pescud overcame severe dyslexia. His accomplishments in life, business, yachting, are extraordinary. Training adults and children with disabilities to participate as crew in the Sydney Hobart Yacht Race, a triumph for all concerned. Many invisible and visible challenges confront severe dyslexics or dyspraxics and deaf individuals. Doubts about our ability can hinder overcoming such challenges, preventing access to the wider community. David's success is documented in a book by Helen O'Neil — *Life Without Limits.*

While many dyslexics cannot read of his adventures, word spread. He is an inspiration.

What about women who are good problem solvers? Where are the books documenting the experiences and challenges posed to women by dyslexia and dyspraxia?

Since beginning writing on this topic so many undiagnosed dyslexic women have come to my notice. Many of them ignore spelling. They have succeeded in spite of dyslexia, using their intelligent and creative minds. Raising children. One ran an art gallery. Fought, or been ignored by the educational system. Living rich rewarding lives. Many have successfully accessed Australian universities with great success. These are the true heroes. So are others who have spent years being told how unsuccessful they are, and yet soldiering on. What is normal? Comparing a bright, dyslexic to a normal child is discrimination.

Penelope Janu, in her novel *Up On Horse Shoe Hill*, writes about a dyslexic heroine who has friends who do her paperwork for her farrier business. Some parents and teachers compare individuals seen as 'not normal' to a perfectionist type of reality, failing to recognise genius and intelligence in others who learn differently. Why is not the individual tested for different ways of learning in kindergarten or when starting school?

Filing Follies

Filing becomes effortless in an already established filing system. Guidelines are clear. Establishing a filing system for personal use is a different matter. Filing becomes a minefield. Financial, medical papers slip in between folders of poems. Short stories languish behind written notes. Photographs linger in boxes out of the way. Family historical material hides in box files of differing colours marching along bookshelves. Contents are always a surprise when decluttering. Textbooks mingle on shelves with fiction. History books have shelves to themselves. Non-fiction books emerge from surprising places. Books arrive, read, kept or discarded. Many fiction books are passed on. Library books, most covered in plastic made from petrochemicals, are allergenic for me. Filing material on computers, for me, can be a gamble. Memory sticks a puzzle. What does each stick have on file? 'Easy,' you say. 'Keep a record.' Where is the book with the record of memory stick contents? 'Always put everything in the same place.' All very well, until you forget. As a child, leaving a book unattended on a chair was fatal. The book would appear back in the rightful position in a bookcase. Molly was a tidiness freak. My mind has always worked better in chaos than in a straightjacket of neatness. Angus claims our untidiness is a reaction to Molly's zealous fastidiousness. He claims she is responsible for us being a tad untidy.

Unanswered Questions

On a personal level, why was my poor spelling ignored by English teachers? Why is it possible for me to read because of phonics? Why is phonics unreliable as a spelling tool? How does one help dyslexics who are unable to use phonics? What did the principal mean when she told Molly on one of my reports, 'The only thing wrong with Claire is her right hand. Fix it.'

Why were dangling sentences not explained to me at Penleigh?

Molly would never know I was dyslexic or dyspraxic. Would knowing the truth have alleviated her shame?

Boys are more likely to be dyslexic than girls. Really? The number of older women who have dyslexic symptoms never ceases to amaze me. What difference does gender make to diagnosis?

As a mature age student, success came with a double major in a Bachelor of Arts Degree. Why was

I helped at university, not at school? Fred apologised for not providing me with the opportunity to continue my education as a teenager. Raising the question, would I have been able to cope with a full-on degree course plus undiagnosed dyslexia? Why do many universities in Australia aid dyslexics?

Why do many schools and universities ignore dyslectic challenges?

Why is the educational and medical world silent about dyspraxia? What harmful choices are made by dyspraxic children who are undiagnosed?

Speech therapists are essential as are exercises, such as Pilates, to build core strength and stabilise balance problems. It seems dyspraxia is invisible. Is diagnosis and the cost of correcting the problem too hard or expensive for the relevant authorities? Why does Australia lag behind the rest of the world in diagnosing and aiding kindergarten and school students who experience dyslexia? We are over 20 years behind the rest of the world.

Infamously, in 1979, a Senate report decided that there was no such condition as dyslexia, poor reading was the result of poor teaching, affecting government funding for the problem of dyslexia. Universities in Australia were forced by legal action to recognise dyslexia and accordingly some have come to the aid of dyslexic students. Why does the Australian government fail to provide more individual aides and equipment for all dyslexic students?

Politicising phonics on the conservative side, with teachers who feel they need to decide how to teach English on the other (according to a recent article in an *Age* 'Good Weekend').

How can these attitudes benefit dyslexic children?

My Writing

Words. I have always loved the sounds. Listening to recitation, changes to the rhythm of words. Rhyming words caress my ears. Sung words are even better. Hymns of praise make my heart sing. Oral storytelling is music to my ears. Phonics, the music of spelling and reading aloud, vowel and syllables creating harmonies.

Piano playing — creating rivers of joyful sound.

Over 30 years' membership with the Western Union Writers. Monthly meetings on the second Friday in the month. Sharing writing news. Reading our work to other members is very enjoyable. Being brave enough to participate in public poetry readings. Enjoying listening to other writers read their own works. Shakespeare's words a journey into a verbal wonderland.

Such a fascination in listening to spoken words. A contrast with my writing difficulties and experiences. Over the last 33 years, the Western Union Writers have been listening to my poems and stories, while sharing their stories with each other. Sending my written work to competitions or magazines has been difficult, if not impossible. Few copies of my work are given to the group because of all the spelling problems. This is my fifth book that has reached the stage of a completed first draft. All have been edited. Now is the time for retyping and self-publishing. A book of Butterfly Mind poems accompanies this book, helping in some way for others to understand the challenges, inspiration, creativity and problem solving. Writing, for me, is a very healing experience. The trauma of dyspraxia, humiliation and shame of being a poor speller, never vanish. However, they often are worked through. Writing deprives traumatic events of their power over emotions, leaving me with the power to choose.

Without my dyslexic butterfly mind, dyspraxia would have been overwhelming. Writing poems about verbal abuse is much easier than including stories about them in a book.

An extract from my poem 'Words that Haunt':

>'You will never amount to anything'
>Bullets attack my self-esteem
>Assaulted my brain
>Lodged in my mind
>Fred's contribution
>'Don't be so bloody stupid.'

>*Claire Moore 21/11/20*

Blessings

I knew my life was full of challenges. Assuming other people had similar lives to mine, the thought of life being hard seemed irrelevant. The challenges I faced served to make me tougher. More able to cope. My cousins were all so much older, I imagined myself in a non-winnable race to catch up with them. Discipline given to me by both Molly and Fred has at times been a salvation. Molly and Fred found it difficult to cope with a sensitive child.

Constantly facing differing levels of frustration with my writing is not easy.

Writing this book has been very confronting and challenging. My mind struggles with structure and essential edits that are a blessing.

Dyslexia can be frustrating and infuriating but not physically painful.

Dyspraxia is an equal challenge but the results of a fall can be very painful, necessitating sudden changes in behaviour.

Puzzlement and frustration because of not being able to recognise when I try too hard. The resultant falls or dyslexia mistakes are definitely not blessings.

How is dyslexia a blessing?

Learning phonics taught to me by Molly through storytelling, poem recitation and tongue twisters qualifies as a blessing. Luckily phonics was taught at primary school thus reinforcing my ability to read and write, another blessing that allowed me access to a world of stories, poems and pictures. My memory was phenomenal. I remembered poems, stories, articles in school papers. Huge blessings.

All through primary school I could read, write and spell better because of my hour of piano practice a day. Nan's gift of music helped both sides of my brain to communicate. Today piano practice continues to help my brain. Never was I labelled dumb or stupid because of my dyslexia. At a private girls' school I was considered a poor speller but never labelled stupid. Another blessing. I continued on in denial of any problem.

Diagnosis of dyslexia helped me to complete a double major arts degree.

For me a huge blessing. Further academic studies at university were too hard. Also in retrospect a blessing as I was able to study other modalities.

Working with other dyslexic beings I noticed that most were humiliated by being unable to read, write or spell. I was blessed with no humiliation. Falling through the cracks enabled me to grow academically without the prism of dyslexia.

Dyslexia has forced me to look at different levels of awareness and being.

Dyslexia does not define who I am. I functioned for years without being aware of this problem. My use of words expands as I replace words I wish to use in a sentence with similar words that are easier to spell.

The chaos caused by my dyslexia has opened my mind up to different solutions and ideas. Given me more compassion for others with similar and different problems.

My mind has learnt to live with imperfection and find alternative solutions.

A game I play.

Dyspraxia undiagnosed achieved what I never could, release from physical exercises and sport classes. Giving me four extra periods a week to study. A huge blessing!

Twenty years of Pilates exercises plus twice daily Dragon Gate Chi Gong exercises have aided my body, blessings in themselves.

Exercise unending is essential to improve my balance.

Diagnosis of dyspraxia was a blessing in disguise forcing me to adopt ways of coping to minimise falls.

The downside is still no conception of my body in space. Continual frustrations.

Falls diminished. Never have I feared falls.

The mantra 'Get up and get on with it' has been invaluable in my battle with my body.

Dyslexia and dyspraxia have blessed me with an improved understanding of human needs. An appreciation of difference encouraging me to be more tolerant of others' differences. Increased my compassion for all who are different who challenge societies rigid standards.

'Disabled? No.'

'Different? Yes.'

Difference became a cause to celebrate.

Dyslexia and dyspraxia have blessed me by helping solve, understand and unravel the never-ending mystery of me.

Acknowledgements

Hazel Edwards, an inspiring writing teacher and mentor who suggested that I write this book.

Johanna Saunders who rescued my email problems in connection with Hazel Edwards' Zoom meeting expert who was always encouraging.

Compliments to Johanna for retyping my manuscript and her first edit.

Margaret Campbell who listened over the telephone to all the stories included and discarded in this book. Her welcome advice a great help.

Sophia Kovachevich, editor par excellence for her excellent editing skills.

Survivor of the final edit!

Helen Cerne, who as a structural editor introduced me to widow sentences, orphan titles and a whole world of structure.

Artist Janice Davis, a huge thank you for kindly donating her painting of a butterfly for use on the front and back cover of this book.

John Moore put up with all the drama. Detective on missing computer files and message sticks. Corrector of final spelling mistakes.

A huge thank you to everyone whose acts made this publication possible. Including all the Hazel nuts in my group.

Thank you to Chris Ringrose.

And thank you to Dalida and Sylvie from BookPOD in helping me bring this book from manuscript to print.

Bibliography

Baker, Jordan (6 March 2021), 'Life Lessons: 'How Learning to Read Became a New Battleground in the Culture Wars — and the Kids caught in the crossfire', p. 8—11; *The Age* 'Good Weekend'

Campbell, Don (2000), *The Mozart Effect for Children*, Hodder Headline, Sydney, NSW

Carper, Jean (2000), *Your Miracle Brain,* Harper Collins, New York

Collins, Dr Anita (2020), *The Music Advantage*, Allen & Unwin, Sydney, Melbourne, Auckland

Davis, Ronald D, with Braun, Eldon M, *The Gift of Dyslexia,* 1st Pub. Ability Workshop Press, Burlingame, California 1994; Souvenir Press 1st Brit ed., London 1995

Dufty, David (2020), *Radio Girl* (pp. 243—258) Allen & Unwin, Sydney, Melbourne, Auckland, London

Dyspraxia Foundation (DCD) 'Definition of Dyspraxia', British Dyslexia Association, 19/3/2023

Goddard, Sally (2002), *Reflexes, Learning and Behavior*, Fern Ridge Press, Eugene, Oregon, USA

Green, Dr Christopher, and Chee, Dr Kit (1994, 1995,1996,1997), *Understanding ADHD*, Doubleday, Sydney, Auckland, Toronto, New York

Hope, Margaret, (1984), *I Would if I Could: Understanding Clumsiness in Children* (pp. 29—33.), Prince of Wales Children's Hospital

Hornsby, Dr Bevé (1984), *Overcoming Dyslexia*, Methuen, Nth Ryde, NSW

Hunter, Ian, Editor: Muhvich, Barbara (1986), *Brain Injury: Tapping the Potential Within*, Hill of Content, Melbourne

International Dyslexia Association, 'Definition of dyslexia', Definition Consensus Project 2023

Janu, Penelope (2019), *Up on Horseshoe Hill*, Mira/Harper Collins, Sydney, NSW

Jorm, AF (First Pub.1983), *The Psychology of Reading and Spelling Disabilities*, Routledge & Kegan Paul, London

MacDonald, Theodore (1984), *First Aid in Reading, Writing and Spelling*, Hale & Iron Monger, Sydney, NSW

O'Neil, Helen (2003), *Life Without Limits: The David Pescud Story* (p. 154), Bantam Books, Sydney, Auckland, Toronto, New York

Promislow, Sharon, Illustrator: Levan, C (1998), *Making the Brain Body Connection*, Kinetic Publishing Corp., Vancouver BC, Canada

Smith, Corinne, Strick, Lisa (1999), *Learning Disabilities A—Z*, Fireside Book, New York

Smelt, Elsie (1983, 1984, 1985), *Complete Guide to English Spelling: A New Approach*, Longman Cheshire, Melbourne

Tolman, Don, *Farmacist Desk Reference, Encyclopedia of Whole Food Medicine, Volume II* (pp. 397—398), Benacquista Publishing Inc and x2x Ltd USA & Hong Kong

Topsfield, Jewel, 'Dyslexia: The Hidden Disability', *The Age*, Saturday (July 2014)

Wagner, Rudolf F, *Dyslexia and Your Child: A Guide for Teachers and Parents*, Chapter 10 'Dyslexia and the Adolescent', pp. 150—153, Revised edition 371.914 WAGN Werribee Library

Zauner, Renate, Translator: Ray, Susan (1980), *Speaking of: Children's Posture Problems and the Injuries They Cause*, Delair Publishing Company, New York

www.ingramcontent.com/pod-product-compliance
Lightning Source LLC
Chambersburg PA
CBHW060133100426
42744CB00007B/767